Advanced Praise For **Adapt. Or Die.**

"What can I say about Kurt Baumberger? He's a master strategist. And strategy is everything. This book will tell you why."

> Sam Unwin, Vice-President of Marketing, Exxon-Mobil Corporation

"Filled with clever insights, engaging ideas, and delightful anecdotes. This book is a wise and amusing guide to the errors of Dealerships that can only be drawn from Kurt's decades of experience."

> Lee McEnany Caraher, Founder and President, Double-Forte

"This book is not simply about marketing; it is about how to choose the right objective performance measurements and stops the madness of Dealerships deploying tactics in search of a strategy. If you read it and follow its lessons, you'll drive your sales, and, more important, your profits!"

> Dr. Chris Moorman, Marketing Strategy Senior Professor, Duke University

"*Adapt Or Die* shows how – much more than we care to admit – Dealers make foolish, and sometimes disastrous, mistakes. Fortunately, this book gives us the solutions we need with a simple to understand, easy to execute process."

> Peter Hennessy, Hennessy Automotive

Adapt. Or Die.

HOW THE INTERNET IS DESTROYING DEALER PROFITS AND WHAT TO DO ABOUT IT

By KURT BAUMBERGER

Publishers Note. This publication is designed to provide accurate and authoritative information in regard to the subject matter covered. It is sold with the understanding that the publisher is not engaged in rendering legal, accounting, or other professional service. If legal advice or other expert assistance is required, the services of a competent professional person should be sought.

Baumberger, Kurt, 1961-

> Adapt. Or Die.: how the internet is destroying dealer profits and what to do about it / Kurt Baumberger.

ISBN 978-0-557-26569-5

1.Business.   2. Economics.   I. Title

Printed in the United States of America; Set in Times New Roman; Printed on acid-free paper

This book is dedicated to my father-in-law

Larry Leser – without whom nothing in my past twenty years

would have been possible

Acknowledgements

In giving advice, seek to help, not please, your friend.

-Solon, Greek statesman, law maker, poet.

My thanks to all the Dealerships and their professionals who helped me with this book. Dealership customers demand more and more every day and these people always answer the call. Special thanks to the AutoNation, Asbury, Hendrick, Penske Automotive Groups who continuously rise to the challenge of leading the industry.

Thanks to Steve Jobs, Larry Ellison and Steve Ballmer and the other technologists that I've had the privilege of discussing ideas in always vibrant exchanges. And thanks to the great Marketers at Apple, HP, Microsoft, P&G, Nike, The Coca-Cola Company, Wendy's, Kraft, Electronic Arts, Nokia, and countless others that I'm proud to have worked with over the years.

It is an honor to be a member of the Duke Basketball Family who continuously adapt to change. Coach K, Dawkins, Collins, Wojo, Carrawell, James, Stephens, Schrage, along with Mike Cragg, Jose Fonseca, Rachel Curtis, Gerry Brown, Mickie K, Debbie K, and Marleah Rogers are some of the finest people that the good Lord ever put on this earth. I hope this book rises to the Duke level of excellence.

And special thanks to Larry Leser and PJ Smith who steadfastly stood by when things got rough. This is a case where when the going got tough, the tough got going.

To the angels in my world, Katie and Griffin, you have brought more joy into my life than you can possibly imagine. Every time I see you the love is overwhelming.

And, lastly, to Sharon, my wife and best friend, who has had doubts, worries, and concerns but stuck it out. Thanks for bearing with me. Always remember the words in our wedding song, "In my mind, we can conquer the world. Together. You and I."

If you think you can or if you think you can't. You're right.

Henry Ford

Contents

PART 3: GET IT DONE

PART 4: MEASURE, REFINE, REPEAT

FOREWORD

Throughout my career spanning from Dealer Specialties to Reynolds & Reynolds to E-Commerce at Asbury Automotive Group, I've interacted with and visited thousands of Dealerships. So I know that our industry is filled with well-meaning, good people who are eager to grow their skills and sales. All they need is the right vision, a solid strategy to follow and strong leadership to build a 21st Century profitable Dealership.

Fortunately, this book delivers everything that's needed. It provides the clearest, cleanest path for Dealers to both understand the new economy and how to take full advantage of it. Dealers who heed this advice and successfully implement these strategies will be in a unique situation – they will have wrestled control back from customers because they will have ceded control; they will find themselves crowned as the automotive thought leaders because they will have deferred to the expertise of others.

I know this seems counter-intuitive. But we work in an industry that's full of contradictions. For instance, why does the average salesperson with dozens and dozens of leads still retail under eight units a month? Why do Dealerships invest hundreds of hours in training yet turnover continues to plague the industry? Why do thousands of technology solutions exist to eliminate costs but margins continue to shrink while advertising expenses per vehicle continue to rise?

The good news is that this book gives you a step by step process to set up your Dealership for success. The strategies are simple. The technology solutions already exist. The implementation takes only a few weeks. The process is market tested. The results are proven.

The bad news is that our automotive industry past, our attitudes and our reliance on "tactics without strategy" prevent us from achieving the profitable sales we desperately want and need. In my experience, Dealer Principals continue to be held hostage by their past success. Just because Dealer Principals were successful selling cars a certain way in 1987 or 1998 or 2003, Dealer Principals often feel that "rolling up your sleeves" and working harder is the answer.

But if the awful "aught" decade taught us anything, it's that today is radically different than yesterday. It's foolish to assume that today's customers will behave like customers did five years ago.

Today's customers cannot be manipulated by sales "methods of control." Customers are not just finding your Dealership in a different way, they act differently because they are different, and what's worse is they are now in control.

Customers have access to your invoice price, your available incentives and the value of their trades. More important, every one of them has a keyboard and they're not afraid to use it!

Customers are using their keyboards to tell the world what they think of you, how they were treated and whether anyone should ever do business with you. They can make or break you – and you have little or no control.

So maybe you've tried a couple of tactics to adapt to this new consumer environment. Maybe you tried a BDC or one-tier pricing, or a couple of CRM campaigns. After all, the car business is full of tactics to help us combat this and to sell that. There are tactics we're taught by our OEMs. There are tactics we get from our 20-Group.

But the problem is not the tactics, it's that we implement them with no vision, no strategy. We are so busy putting on band-aids that we have no time to fix our broken leg. That's exactly why this book is so valuable – it not only cures our broken leg but also provides rigorous physical therapy to make us stronger than ever before.

Before we can get well, we have to want to be well. We must be willing to unshackle ourselves from the past, cede control to customers, and act strategically in this digital age of tactics. It's all right here in this book.

The only question left unanswered is whether you have the courage to Adapt. Or Die.

Steve Stauning, Kain-Stauning

PREFACE

Over the past few years, I've seen millions of dollars spent, misspent, and overspent by Automotive Dealers trying to transform their Dealerships to adapt to the Internet. And I've noticed predictable patterns in the way Dealers try to design, build, and implement these adaptations. On the whole, they make similar mistakes, reach similar conclusions, and make similar decisions.

If you are a Dealer or GM or Internet Manager, you've probably done the same things. But forewarned is forearmed, and it's helpful to know what works and what doesn't.

This book is based on firsthand experience working with hundreds of Dealers. Those who listened and adapted to the requirements of the Internet made a lot of money. They checked their pride, cynicism and "not invented here" attitude at the door and opened their minds to innovation and new thinking. Some of these Dealerships used Marketing tools I developed for My Dealer Broadcast and others hired my firm for consulting or training.

Regardless of the relationship, I've learned something priceless from every Dealership. It is this collective wisdom that you'll find in these pages. And there's no need to read this book from cover to cover. Each chapter makes sense on its own.

What's important is to have the courage to be honest with yourself. It's tempting to exaggerate your successes and minimize your shortcomings. That does no good to anyone. You can use the processes in Part 3 to help you honestly assess not what should happen or what you hope happens, but what actually happens in your Dealership.

This is called a "How To" book for a reason. Automotive Dealerships are going through a business model transition where survival is not assured. Customer behavior has irreversibly changed and your Dealership must move aggressively move in a disciplined fashion. In short, "Adapt. Or Die." Just as the engineers on Apollo 13 addressed unprecedented challenges, you must have the same resolve to "work the problem." What's it going to take to get your Dealership to safely return to profitability?

NASA Apollo 13 Liftoff

This guide will lay out a path for you, but only you can make it happen. Or as Houston Control NASA Flight Director of Apollo 13, Gene Krantz, said to a cynical NASA Manager, "With all due respect, sir, I believe this will be our finest hour."

After all, failure is not an option.

NASA Apollo 13 Crew Upon Safe Return

Exercise:

What are the Top 3 hurdles or obstacles that will prevent you from successfully transforming your "Brick and Mortar" Dealership to a profitable E-Commerce business model?

1. _____
   _____
   _____

2. _____
   _____
   _____

3. _____
   _____
   _____

PART 1

TRUTH HURTS

Introduction:

YOU'RE GOING TO GET ANGRY

This book will make you angry. Then you'll want to argue about what's in it. Then you'll think of clever ways to throw the "b------- flag," especially since you're an entrepreneur that's used to independent thinking. And ultimately, you will try to ignore most of what you'll read. But your heart won't let you. Because you know it's true. And the truth hurts.

You'll probably want to shoot the messenger and that's your choice. But the message won't go away because the facts are irrefutable. You'll say that statistics can be manipulated to make any argument seem plausible. Since that's what politicians do every day and no one trusts them.

But this book is not trying to sell you anything. It is trying to save your Dealership by compiling an exhaustive set of observations, industry trends, and financial facts from a wide variety of sources. To refute the perspective of your industry peers and experts from similar

 retail industries, is equivalent to putting your head in the sand and hoping everything will turn out alright. Well, *hope is not a strategy*.

The good news is that you can learn from other industries and avoid a lot of their mistakes. You are not destined to end up on the dump heap like Circuit City, Linens and Things, Montgomery Ward or K-Mart. But to do so means you need to begin thinking like Amazon, Apple, Dell, Lending Tree and others that are thriving in the E-Commerce world of price wars, "me too" products, and unrelenting customer demands.

Survival Guide

What do these successful companies know that car Dealerships don't? Well, perhaps they understand the true premise of Darwin's "Evolution" theory. Darwin's seminal work is often mistakenly paraphrased as "survival of the fittest." In fact, Darwin postulated that a species survival is the result of *rapid evolution and adaption to environmental change*.

Whether or not these companies have this Darwinian principle embedded in their corporate DNA, they certainly recognized that there were no traditional business models to follow in the rapidly evolving marketplace. Each day brought new challenges and failures, but these companies learned that to survive and thrive they had to continuously and relentlessly overcome failure. They knew they had no choice – Adapt. Or Die.

So what did they do? After all, these companies not only profitably grew through the last two recessions but thrived in the Internet Age. Look at Apple Computer's revenue growth through the most difficult worldwide economic recession since the Great Depression.

Apple Revenue and Net Income (In U.S. $Billions)

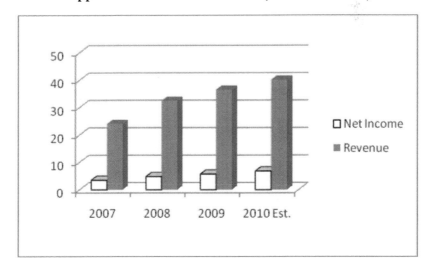

From 2007-2009, customers were overleveraged. Housing values plummeted. Unemployment reached double digits. The banking system nearly collapsed. As a result, customers cut back their spending in record amounts, particularly on "discretionary and luxury goods." Yet, through this economic hurricane, Apple almost doubled its revenue while steadily increasing profits.

What does Apple know that Dealerships don't? First and foremost, Apple understands Marketing. That's Marketing with a capital "M", not a lower case "m." The difference is profound.

Big "M" Marketing defines the strategy that is the heart of everything an organization does. *Marketing defines who you are, what you do, why you do it, and to whom you do it*. That means the real responsibility for marketing belongs to everybody in your organization, particularly the Dealer and his right hand man, the GM.

BIG M_{arketing}

In contrast, lower case marketing is limited in both size and scope of the impact it has on your Dealership. Lower case marketing folks are quite capable of making marketing communication elements such as signs, brochures, and merchandise. They worry about design, color schemes, and production quality, not about creating customer demand for your Dealership.

And it's not sufficient to just go and hire somebody and give them a Marketing title. The reality is that everybody has to be part of Marketing and everybody has to understand the job of selling stuff, positioning stuff, and making sure people buy stuff.

To navigate through the Internet and build an E-Commerce business, it's critical to have a "BIG M" Marketing person in charge. Think about it – your Dealership website is the first impression that you make to 90+% of your customers. It is your primary means to "go to market." It is not a different sales channel, it is THE sales channel.

And who is responsible today? A master Marketer or a salesperson that "gets" computers? Who has Profit and Loss responsibility for your Sales and Fixed Operations E-Commerce businesses? Do they have strategic, operational, and execution responsibility? Do they have specific customer demand objectives to achieve? Do they work on translating demand to preference to purchase?

The person in charge of your E-Commerce businesses is critical, because he/she defines for your Dealership:

- How you compete
- How you communicate
- How you sell
- How you service
- How you deliver products and services

By now, if you are like most Dealers and GM's, you are probably feeling pretty insecure about your ability to be a master Marketer or to hire and work with one. Well, you can rest easy. That's what this book is all about and you'll find resources in Chapter 12 to help you get where you need to go.

What's important is to begin the journey with the end in mind. Stephen Covey wrote in "The 7 Habits of Highly Effective People," that to begin with the end in mind means to start with an understanding of your destination. It's incredibly easy to get caught up in an activity trap and to be busy – very busy – without being very effective.

Arguably, falling into this activity trap is a skill that car Dealerships have perfected – the art of ineffective activity. Walk into any Dealership and you'll see a beehive of activity. Salespeople are busily checking email or entering CRM data, managers are endlessly running sales or financial reports, and GM's are perpetually worrying about how to deliver their bonus based sales numbers.

What is the Dealership destination? Shouldn't all activities be focused on creating customer demand for the Dealership's products and services? Shouldn't all activities be forward-looking instead of backward reflecting?

Well, the destination of this book is to transform your current "Brick and Mortar" Dealership equipped with little more than a "brochure-ware" website to a *fully automated, process driven E-Commerce business where you will sell more to more for more!*

What You Can Expect

The marketing business is replete with jargon. It's easy to get trapped in a marketing conversation loaded with phrases like "investing in awareness to maximize the buyer experience and increase brand relevancy." If you run into someone that uses these phrases, just walk away. They're talking gibberish.

You need to make sure that you evolve your business model strategically with integrated processes and Behavior Tracking or BT. Anything less is merely a collections of various and sundry tactics that add unnecessary complexity to your life.

The jazz great, Charles Mingus, once explained, "Making the simple complex is commonplace; making the complicated simple, awesomely simple, that's creativity."

Charles Mingus, 1962

That's what we'll do in this book. We will describe how customers have wrestled "sales control" away from Dealerships in Part 1. Then, we will look at three simple (yet very creative) business model strategies that you can use in Part 2. Finally, we will put everything together in Part 3 with specific actions to take and resources to contact for help.

But let's make sure it's crystal clear upfront what Marketing won't do:

- ➢ It won't overcome bad products

- ➢ It won't overcome lousy service

- ➢ It won't close the deal

- ➢ It won't compensate for incompetent sales force

- ➢ It won't work overnight

17

So what will Marketing do?

Create customer demand for your Dealership.

And until that happens, nothing happens.

Customer Centricity

So how do you create demand for your Dealership with tons of online "noise" and short attention spans? You start with the customer. You understand what they want. What they need. What they demand. It's not about your products. It's not about your service. And as you'll learn, it isn't even about price. I know that may seem like heresy, but, read on.

Car Dealership advertising has a well earned reputation about being about three people – Me, Myself, and I. How many times have you seen a Dealer or GM get in front of a camera to get customers to "Come On Down"? Do you really think your summer tan line in this kind of ad is going to get customers to cancel their cookout or trip to the beach to go to your Dealership?

No one cares about that stuff other than you and your old college fraternity brothers. Dealerships must center all of their efforts on the customer because a Dealership can't create demand unless it addresses customer needs and wants. If you do that, then you will be able to create enthusiastic demand to do business with your Dealership above all others.

What you'll find on these pages are the "best practices" of great brands like Advil, USA TODAY, Coca-Cola and great businesses like Dell, iTunes and Amazon where I have personally played a role in their success. The insights I gained from these successful experiences and the lessons learned have a direct bearing on today's automotive retail industry.

Fundamentally, what distinguishes these brands and businesses is their unwavering commitment to connect with customers. Whenever I give speeches or teach classes at business schools like Duke and Stanford, I explain that the success of every company is, has been, and always will be in the minds of customers. But it is *your responsibility* to use your E-Commerce technology tools to go to customers and explain why they should do whatever it is that you want them to do.

Yet, every day I hear Dealers, GM's and salespeople moan and complain that every customer comes to your Dealership simply demanding the lowest price. But why are you surprised? What's on your advertising? Price. What's on your website home page? Price. What's painted on your windows? Price.

19

And yet Dealerships are surprised when customers just want to talk about price? Really? Your Dealership just spent a lot of money, time, and effort to reach these customers. Your Dealership had a choice of what to say and you chose to explain to customers that they should ask about price. Congratulations, you've proved that Marketing works and that you can do it!

But you have not explained how your product or service is going to make their life significantly better. You haven't told them what makes your Dealership better than any other. Nor have you given them any reason to believe you. (And trust me, they have a hard time believing you.)

You have not focused on how they perceive Dealership value – *it's not price!* And when you're finished with this book you'll know what is important to them and how to tap into this demand to survive and thrive.

Levers Of The Business

When I was just starting out in my career, Joe Plummer, Senior Vice President of Young & Rubicam Worldwide, got on my subway train as I was heading to uptown Manhattan. At the time, Y&R was the world's largest advertising agency serving clients in more than 50 countries. And Joe was a visionary, brilliant strategic thinker, savvy businessman, and my mentor.

I immediately noticed that Joe was highly agitated. He had just left an Executive Management meeting where the leadership team was trying to figure out how to grow the agency profitably during the recession that the U.S. was experiencing at the time.

He told me that he stormed out of the meeting and was so angry that he couldn't see straight. I was immediately concerned that there might be job cuts and as a junior level person, my head would surely be on the chopping block.

Indeed, the management team was talking about cutting employees to survive and continue to be profitable. Then, the CFO took over the discussion and began to propose severe expense cuts and started to question the spending habits of each department's small expense account budgets.

That's when Joe lost it. Although I still didn't understand why he was so upset since the actions under consideration certainly made sense to me. Then, Joe turned to me and said, "You cannot save your way to prosperity."

He explained that no one in the room understood the levers of the business. When I pressed him for more detail, he explained that every business has two or three things that it controls that can build the business. Then Joe asked me, *"What two or three things can we do to grow our business profitably?"*

In the agency world, one lever was clients with large media budgets. (This was back in the day when agencies were paid 15% on all media purchases.) The second lever was clients on retainer. (These were clients that had pharmaceutical drugs awaiting FDA approval.)

Joe said we needed to form a cross-functional new business group and go after "A, B, C" clients – Airlines, Beer, and Cigarettes. He said we needed to hire a second team with MD's and PhD's to pursue pharmaceutical clients.

That's right. In difficult financial circumstances, Joe wanted to spend money. No client would pay for a new business pitch and those pitches were expensive. And hiring a team of MD's and PhD's was not cheap either. But Joe knew when business is down that's the time to move the levers that would get the agency in a position to win in the long-term.

Next thing I knew, I was on the Tiger Team that landed USAir, Miller Brewing, and Winston cigarettes. We went on to land Advil, Sominex, and a number of other Over-The-Counter (OTC) drugs. And sure enough, the agency doubled in size and profits flowed for years.

So what are the levers of an automotive Dealership today? Not yesterday or in ten years, but today. What are the two or three things that Dealerships can do today to grow the business profitably?

The only place to look is the Dealership's financial statements. Where is the profit? Where is the cost? *How does the Dealership grow one and strip out the other?*

Today, the levers of an automotive dealership are pre-owned sales and Fixed Operations. These are the highest margin and most profitable areas of the Dealership. But how much force is being exerted on these levers of the business?

And if new vehicle sales are a necessary but less profitable part of the business, then how much is being invested to automate the sales process and eliminate the expensive costs of human capital?

Profit Is All That Matters

Since the day the first Dealership opened, the sole focus of the Dealership was to sell new cars. Selling pre-owned cars and providing Fixed Operations service came afterwards as a logical extension of supporting new car sales.

So when the Internet arrived, it seemed to be a logical extension of selling new cars. It was a new advertising medium. You published your vehicles on your website along with some copy about how your Dealership was the best to do business with. Eventually, you added some pictures of your vehicles and hoped that people would wait long enough for the images to populate before the dial up internet connection from America Online broke down.

Fast forward to today, you now know that you can advertise your vehicles with multiple pictures, streaming video, and more information than customers can possibly handle. And you've proven that you can sell both new and pre-owned vehicles over the Internet. *But can you sell cars on the Internet profitably?*

The sole purpose of Marketing is to get more people to buy more of your product, more often, for more money. That's the only reason to spend a nickel. If your Marketing efforts are not delivering customers to the cash register with wallets in their hands to buy your product, *don't do it!*

You need to center all of your Dealership E-Commerce activities to capitalize on the fact that customers love a new car. Customers love the smell of a new car and the value of a pre-owned car. They love to drive around and show off. They love to discover the new features and electronics on a car. Getting a new car or "sweet ride" is a truly magical feeling because, fundamentally a car purchase is an emotional experience. Or, at least, it should be.

So why is the buying process so damn miserable? Why is it adversarial from the beginning to the end? Why do both buyer and seller feel like the other one "beat me down" or "doesn't appreciate me and what I'm trying to do?" Why can't both sides profit in this relationship? Why is the automotive industry the only industry where this visceral distaste exists? (If going on a date – an emotional experience – was as miserable as purchasing a car, there would be zero population growth!)

Before you answer these questions, you must embrace four new premises of doing business today:

1. Dealerships can no longer compromise on E-Commerce capabilities. They must build or buy technology which delivers nothing less than eye-popping innovation.

2. Dealerships can no longer aim for anything less than hassle-free transactions. Customers enjoy effortless, flawless, and instantaneous performance from one industry and want it in the automotive industry.

3. Dealerships can no longer assume that good basic service is enough. Customers demand 24/7 service – and raise their standards continuously.

4. Dealerships can no longer afford to layer on "Brick and Mortar" infrastructure costs to new vehicle purchases. They must change their business model to a more efficient cost structure.

In the buyer-seller relationship, the tables have turned – the buyer is king. Look no further than the computer industry. In the beginning of the PC age, the market had room for legions of new companies. But the party ended when customers figured out that all companies that offered "state-of-the-art" technology were basically the same. Each company was uniformly supplied by Intel, Microsoft, and Seagate so how different could they be?

Customers demanded more, and then still more, and the industry had to adapt or die. Compaq is gone. IBM is gone. SONY cut back to just a few products. The winners are HP, Dell, and Apple. Each a master Marketer. Each customer centric. Each married to a single core strategy. Each focused on E-Commerce process excellence.

Your Dealership is no different. Customers have stripped the profit out of new vehicle sales so you need to invest in processes that will reduce the cost of sales while accelerating inventory turn. You need to identify new processes to exert force on the levers of the business that will grow the business profitably. Because profit is all that matters.

There's No Mystery To Survival

What you're going to see is not a collection of sleight-of-hand tricks or magical silver bullets. No rabbits and no hats. What you're going to find instead is an assortment of new and well-used tools. And not only am I going to let you look at them, am I also going to tell you how I've seen these tools used to sell billions of dollars of goods and services. And I am going to explain why they were used the way they were.

Because I've been in the retail sales and marketing business and working it hard for a quarter of a century, you will benefit from this open dialogue about the whole concept of surviving in a rapidly changing world. I know that a lot of Dealerships are in big trouble today because they are acting on old assumptions. Those assumptions need to be reexamined. I want to challenge you to start that process.

It's been said by many Dealerships "there are a lot of dead pioneers." That's a pretty cynical statement. It implies that doing something new and different is a near certain failure.

I wonder what Leland Stanford would say to this statement. Stanford was literally a U.S. pioneer who recognized that the business landscape in the mid-1800's was rapidly changing his business. Sales and profits at his General Store in Albany, NY were dropping year over year. The population in Albany reached a plateau, new competition entered the market, and fewer homes were being built. Stanford assessed the situation and realized that what worked in the past was not going to work in the future.

So Stanford moved his once profitable General Store to where the buyers were – in Northern California. There were thousands of miners seeking gold and they needed supplies. These buyers needed different products, delivered in different ways, to meet different demands. Stanford didn't simply move the same sales methodologies that worked in Albany, NY to the wild, wild West. He adapted to these new, different buyers and sought to satisfy their unique information, product, delivery and price demands.

He effectively modified his entire "go to market" strategy in order to sell more to more for more. To be able to expand his sales territory and lower his cost of goods, he built the Central Pacific Railroad. To provide financing for his customers, he founded Wells Fargo Bank. To satisfy his customers local transportation needs, he established "The Farm" to breed horses and pack mules.

By adapting to new market conditions, he became so wealthy that he was able to acquire most of the land south of San Francisco. Before his death, he philanthropically founded an institute of higher learning with the stipulation that the students would pursue an education path "for some useful and innovative pursuit." Thus, Stanford University was established in his family's name and the university became the epicenter of Silicon Valley.

Today, economists call this process "Creative Destruction" – the destruction of old economic business models to create new more profitable business models. Creative Destruction is one of the fundamental driving forces of the free enterprise system. New competitors, products, methodologies, technologies all destroy as much (or more) as they create. *It's called progress and it is undeniable.*

In this book, I'm going to present a new point of view to you about how to adapt to your new business model. I'm convinced these ideas are on target. I'm equally convinced they will work for you. In fact, I know they work because I've seen them work for all sorts of Dealerships. Domestic and Import. Rural and Suburban and Urban. Single store and large auto group.

But the ultimate purpose is not to persuade you to agree with my thinking, but rather to chart a new course for your Dealership. I will toss a few grenades – to bust up some entrenched thinking – and there's likely to be some collateral damage. But the intent is to get you

thinking about where you are today and how you are going to get where you need to be tomorrow.

The path is clear:

> Be "Big M" Marketer

> Be strategic (and loyal to that strategy)

> Be execution experts

You will find all you need in these pages. You will be given Subject Matter Experts (SME's) to contact for more information and to answer your questions. Remember that you are fighting for survival so work with deliberate speed using all the tools available to you. Now is not the time to be proud. Asking for help may be your only way to get back to the land of prosperity.

Good luck and good selling!

1

WHY WORK SO HARD?
TO MAKE MONEY

You probably got into this business because you loved cars. Your dealership may be a family business spanning generations. You may love to be a part of your community and get a kick out of sponsoring the local Little League team or enjoy making charitable donations that make a difference in the lives of the less fortunate. These reasons all used to be important to attract customers and build personal relationships. These personal relationships were built on trust. And this deep trust created loyalty.

Think about your Dealership back then. You could get away with simply bonding with your customers. You know the drill – shoot a commercial, throw in a sweet price deal, and blow your monthly budget on some expensive airtime to drive in traffic. You put up banners and balloons. You might have even thrown some hot dogs on the grill. And you got what you needed – warm bodies walking into your multi-million dollar "Brick and Mortar" showroom.

Then, you really got to work. You applied your sales methods of control. You worked with customers until they were putty in your hands. You tantalized them with product information, seduced them with test drives, enticed them with easy financing, and looked them in the eye to assure them that you were treating them fairly and appreciated their business.

In Marketing terms, you were the brand. Your name meant something. In fact, you wanted it to stand for something that differentiated you from all other Dealerships. You wanted to beat the competition with the best product, people, process, and delivery.

And ten years ago, 80% of U.S. car buyers were satisfied with the vehicle buying process according to the annual Capgemini Cars Survey. But this same annual survey reports that _less than 20% of U.S. car buyers are satisfied today._ What changed? The Internet.

No One Will Be Spared

Before the Internet changed retailing forever, the biggest change had been the slow erosion of locally owned independent retailer to national "Big Box" chains. Thirty years ago, it was common to go to the local druggist, stop by and look at the puppy

in the local pet store, drop by a local record store to hear the latest tunes, and walk into the local stereo store to dream about your next set of killer speakers.

Then, the "Big Box Boys" invaded, slowly but steadily changing Main Street as we knew it. Wal-Mart, Target, CVS and others destroyed the Five and Dime stores and pharmacies. Home Depot and Lowe's laid the lumber yards and hardware stores to waste. PetSmart wiped out the local pet store. Best Buy and others crushed all "mom and pop" customer electronics retailers.

Fast forward to today and now the "Big Box Boys" are being driven out of business. Look at the list of retailers that no longer exist or are facing bankruptcy: Circuit City, Linens and Things, Borders, Ritz Camera, Big 10 Tire, Crabtree and Evelyn, Bi-Lo, K-Mart, Blockbuster. *The Internet forced them to lower prices to compete, but they could (or wouldn't) adapt their business model to adapt.*

There were plenty of warning signs. In the late 1990's, Dell introduced a new Sales Model that revolutionized the computer retail experience and virtually wiped out all the independent and even some chain retailers like CompUSA. Dell's innovation was to automate the entire sales process: Make Selection, Determine Price, Add Accessories and Finance Purchase.

Sound familiar? These are the same basic steps in automotive retailing. They are the same basic steps in any retail process. Dell recognized this process and created multi-media content, "What's this?" pop-up explanations, start to finish workflow, and real-time shopping cart pricing calculations. And before long customers to became comfortable configuring a $1,000 computer or $70,000 server system. It worked because Dell made it straight forward, automated, and user friendly.

Amazon took the process a step further by building a knowledge base that sends outbound recommendations to you based on your previous purchase behavior. More important, Amazon lets customers provide their own ratings, product reviews, wish lists, and recommendations to others. So now customers are involved in a cooperative partnership with a retailer. In effect, they are an extended sales force for Amazon and they cost nothing. And free is always in the budget!

The power has permanently shifted away from the retailer to the customer for the first time in retailing history. With the touch of a key on a computer or the tap of a screen on an iPhone, customers can find what they want, where they want it, at the price they are willing to pay with the delivery they can choose. Now that customers control the purchasing process, retailers are never going to get it back.

That Was Then And This Is Now

Well, as my German farmer father likes to say, "That was then and this is now. So now what are you going to do?" And a lot of Dealerships just don't get it.

There are still commercials flooding the airwaves with messages that no one listens to any more. There are "Tent Sales" and "Football Fall

Fever" events that no one attends. And don't forget the number of trees destroyed for direct mail that generates a .001% response.

Dealerships who think that they "get it" go into rhapsodies about a new website, new CRM, more efficient financing process, or better trained sales force. These Dealerships genuinely believe these isolated tactics are really going to help the business grow or boost profits.

But those aren't the things that boost sales and profits. You don't make any money until you sell cars, and you can't sell cars until you've gotten people to want to do business with you and conduct transactions the way they want them to be transacted.

Dealerships aren't getting the job done today or you would be beating your competition to a pulp. You'd have traffic streaming into your door to buy cars and your Fixed Operations would be overwhelmed. Your expenses would be dropping and your profit would be rising. Cash would be flowing throughout the Dealership.

Here's a table of some of the things that used to work and why they don't work anymore. (Just to be clear – if you are doing any of these things, _stop immediately!_ You're wasting precious resources of time, effort, and money.)

	"Brick & Mortar"	"Virtual"	Difference
Build Awareness	Manufacturer Advertising Editorial PR Car Shows	OEM Websites Lead Provider Behavior Tracking	Then: Untracked Now: 100% Trackable

Generate Traffic	Local Newspaper, Radio, TV	SEM, SEO CRM Campaigns	Then: One to Many Now: One to One
Set Appointments	Phone Voicemail Email	Automated Scheduling	Then: Manual Process Now: Fully Automated
Make Selection	Inventory Lot Walk Walk-Around Test Drive	Online Configuration Virtual 360° Streaming Video	Then: 3.8 Visits Now: 1.3 Visits
Negotiate Price	Newspaper Ad Pricing Protracted Negotiations Undisclosed Final Price Fees	Online Price Comparisons No Hassle Prices Complete Transparency	Then: 5-6 Hours Now: 1 Hour
Assess Trade	Trade-in Integral to Sale Valuation Negotiation	Separate Transaction Market Determined	Then: Unpredictable Now: Scheduled
Sell Financing	Paper Based Few F&I Options	Online Approval Pre-qualified	Then: Bad Credit Now: Qualified Buyers

Adapt or Die

Just like the Ice Age suddenly killed the dinosaurs roaming the earth, the Internet is quickly killing the "Big Box Boys" and retailing will never be the same again. The speed of online innovation is unprecedented in human history. In 2006, TIME magazine made its annual selection of "man, woman, or idea that for better or worse have most influence events of the preceding year" and named "YOU" as "Man of the Year." TIME magazine editors recognized that customers were now in control of journalism, popular culture, art, and, yes, retailing.

Today, the battle for customers has certainly shifted out of the Dealership showroom and on to the Internet. The product information stranglehold that Dealerships once enjoyed is long gone. Product, promotion, and price information that was once the sole province of the Dealership showroom is now splashed all over the Internet. Now the battle starts online in the "hearts and minds" of customers where a positive perception must be created for the Dealership to be under "purchase consideration."

In other industries, retailers that waited to see how everything was going to pan out were wiped out. Dealerships need to learn from these mistakes and move fast or be left behind. It's not a matter of waiting to see how the chips might fall. Speed is critical.

Just look at how media is consumed today and how fast these innovations became mainstream. It's not a matter of decades. It's a matter of months. In less than twelve months, the Apple App Store has over 100,000 applications. In the first six months after the release of Amazon's Kindle, 1 million downloads occurred.

New Media	Brand Name	Birth Year
Digital Music Downloads	iPod	2001
Digital Video Recorders	TiVo	2002
Streaming Video	YouTube	2005
E-Readers	Kindle	2007
Smart Phone Applications	App Store	2008
WiMax	Clear	2009

"Old Media" companies like newspapers, magazines, radio stations and even the huge television networks took their time to adapt. Now many of these media companies are either extinct – Seattle Courier, Rocky Mountain News, Christian Science Monitor, Red Herring – or are facing bankruptcy.

And how fast is your Dealership adapting to this incredibly changed environment?

Coach Mike Krzyzewski, head coach of Olympic Gold Medal winner Team USA and three-time NCAA National Champion Duke University, explains that he has a distinct advantage over most businesses since he must take stock of his team (i.e., his business) at least once a year. Kids graduate (or head to the NBA). New freshmen arrive. Kids improve their skills over the summer. He's got to adapt to this changed environment in order to keep winning.

More important, Coach K recognizes that what has worked in the past, won't necessarily work in the future. When he started coaching, he won with a great center and quick guards. Then, he won with deadly three-point shooters. Now, the strict man-to-man defense that Coach K perfected is often shelved for a zone defense. Each year there was a new environment and he continuously wins because he continuously adapts.

But most Dealers and GM's rarely take a step back every year and consciously consider how they will change their "go to market" approach in order to win. For instance, how have Dealerships overhauled their sales process to handle the fact that 90+% of customers today will extensively use the Internet to do research before they walk into a dealership?

How have Dealerships incorporated Behavior Tracking (or BT) in their Internet infrastructure? Behavior Tracking can tell you for any specific customer what was viewed, when, and how. Behavior Tracking can alert your Dealership that a specific customer (name, phone number, email, year, make, model) is engaged with your Dealership online.

How have Dealerships automated follow up to customers that customized to the unique needs of each individual customer? This is routinely done at Amazon where a customer gets a long set of recommended items to purchase based on their unique interests.

Yet, many Dealerships have computers from the mid 1990's. What's more, these ancient computers are often locked down in a painfully slow Internet network. If Dealership folks can barely access their own website, then how do you expect your Dealership to ever win in that kind of environment? How can the Dealership win consistently? How can the Dealership achieve any standard of excellence?

You must simply Adapt. Or Die.

Exercise:

Is your Dealership doing what's necessary to win?

	Yes	No
Do you invest the same amount of people, time and money on your "Virtual Showroom" as you do on your "Brick and Mortar" showroom?	O	O
Do you conduct an annual Internet assessment benchmarking your Dealership performance against "Best Practices"?	O	O
Do you prepare an annual Internet Business Plan including a Profit and Loss budget?	O	O
Do you utilize Behavior Tracking to separate Internet Leads into "Hot. Or Not." groupings?	O	O
Do you routinely invest in technology training such as monthly skill building?	O	O
Do you automate reports, "to do" tasks, and customer alerts to maximize sales effectiveness?	O	O

If you answered "no" to any of these questions, then your Dealership is not prepared to win in today's customer controlled environment. Continue reading to see what you can do to adapt.

2

SET UP TO FAIL AND DOING IT FABULOUSLY!

Maybe the goal of religious mystics is to live purely in the present, but a Dealership always has to be planning what to do tomorrow. That's because no matter what you have done to get you where you are today, you are going to have to do something different tomorrow. No matter how successful you've been, there's no resting on your laurels.

But what makes change so urgent now? The doomsayers and dark clouds have massed many times before over the automotive industry. Change, challenge, and crisis have all become clichés. A steady hand on the Dealership wheel has always worked before. It's all about good people and good processes. Surely these balms will work again.

Remember hearing these rationalizations?

> "It's really not a very good value, because it doesn't include a lot of our features." That's what American Airlines said about Southwest Airlines policy of providing no meals, no reserved seating, and no long flights.

> "It's a good value but not our preferred customer market." GM, Chrysler, and Ford ignored Honda and Toyota because it entered the "basic transportation" segment of the market.

> "People want to touch, feel or listen before they buy." That's what booksellers and record store owners said about Amazon.com.

Eventually, of course, the signs of a failing value proposition cannot be ignored. Dealerships have seen growth stall, margins shrink, and customers take flight. As the slide in profits turns into a free fall, Dealers scramble, resorting to a series of quick fixes to bolster near-term performance. These actions, all too familiar, are ineffective, cynical efforts that veil a Dealership's declining value to customers. The initiatives treat the symptoms, rather than the root causes of the poor performance.

Compound this lack of value proposition with manufacturer bankruptcies, government intervention, closed dealerships, and a crippling economy. Then, mix in a financial system teetering on the brink of worldwide disaster and you've got the perfect storm.

But there are glimpses of sunlight peering through the clouds and demand for vehicles will increase if for no other reason than older vehicles will break down and wear out. So unless Spock and Scottie from Star Trek create, launch, and commercialize transporter technology in the next few years, people will be returning to purchase cars and trucks again. (Although I wouldn't bet against Spock and Scottie, especially if Captain Kirk is pushing the project!)

The question is whether you are ready to survive in the new Internet world order. Let me use a comprehensive study of over one million Internet Leads to show you what I mean about being ready to survive. This study compared one million Internet Leads with actual Motor Vehicle Department records to see what the Internet Leads actually did. And the results confounded everyone.

For instance, there is a widely held belief that only about 10-15% of Internet Leads actually buy a vehicle within 60 days of submitting their inquiry for more information. In fact, 55% of Internet Leads purchased a vehicle. So if your Dealership is only closing 10-15% of your Internet Leads, then your Dealership *"blows through" 40% of its Internet Leads!*

You might argue that these Internet Leads actually never intended to buy from you. Well, the fact of the matter is that you simply didn't give them enough reasons to buy from you. Because 20% of your Dealership's Internet Leads bought the same make (new) from a different Dealership. Another 10% bought the same make (pre-owned) from a different Dealership. Another 20% bought a competitive make from a different Dealership.

So your Dealership blew through three types of Internet Leads that could have and should have been yours!

Internet Lead Buying Behavior (First 60 Days)

☐ Buy From Competition

■ Buy From You

▨ Aren't Ready To Buy

Source: Buying Influence Study, 2008

Deals Left On The Table

This is one of those times where you are going to want to ignore the data or throw the "B------- flag." Because the data says that unless you are closing 45% of your Internet Leads, then you are leaving deals on the table. You're no doubt scrolling through your mind all of the money you've spent and things you've tried in order to sell more cars over the Internet. And since you've failed, the data must be wrong.

Resist the temptation. The data is accurate and irrefutable. Dig deeper into the data and you'll see exactly where the problems arise. Dealerships are failing fabulously to meet customers' fundamental needs. This is another one of those places where the truth hurts.

Customer Wants...	But Customer Gets...
Attention	30% Leads Completely Ignored
Immediate Response	5.4 Hour Average Response
Detailed Product Information	80% No Product Information
Detailed Price Information	75% No Price Information
Product Availability	70% No Availability Information

With this level of performance, it's hardly surprising that Dealerships only sell to 10-15% of Internet Leads. Frankly, it's almost a miracle Dealerships sell anything at all!

And take a look at the kind of responses going out to these Internet Leads. Remember that these customers have volunteered personal information to you and asked for a business relationship. They are literally inviting you into their home, business, and life. And here are some real-life examples of how your guests are treated:

> "Thanks for your inquiry. Someone will call you to follow up within the next 24-48 hours."

> "We appreciate your business at (Blank). It's our pleasure to serve you. Unfortunately, I'm with another customer and will get back to you as soon as possible."

> "Welcome to (Blank). We look forward to seeing you in our showroom where you can experience the thrill of driving a (Blank). In the meantime, if you have any questions, please feel free to call me."

Now imagine if this customer was a walk-in and your showroom floor salespeople gave the same kind of answer. Suppose your salesperson sauntered up to a customer that's interested in buying from your Dealership and says, "I'll get to you when I'm good and ready." Or "I'm busy." Or "I know you want to do business with us, but I need you to conform to a sales process that's convenient for me."

How fast would you fire them? How loud would you be yelling? And what would you say to the surviving salespeople? You'd probably jump on your soapbox and give a speech something like this Seven-Step Sales Process:

1. Greet them by name
2. Welcome them to the showroom
3. Start to assess their needs
4. Educate them on our products and services
5. Do a walk-around to help them make a selection
6. Take them on a test drive
7. Ask for their business

Now you may have more steps or different steps that work for your Dealership, but why do you treat "Brick and Mortar" showroom customers better than "virtual showroom" customers? Why don't you apply the lessons learned in the "Brick and Mortar" world to the virtual world? In fact, why don't you _insist_ that the lessons learned in the showroom be replicated in the virtual world?

Customers Choose With Their Feet

There's an old retailing adage that customers choose with their feet – meaning foot traffic in the store tells the retailer if he or she is meeting customer needs. Well, here's some more truth that hurts.

Foot traffic (i.e., non-Internet customers) into Dealer Showrooms has been in decline for almost two decades. That's right. Declining foot traffic is not a recent phenomenon due to the struggling U.S. economy.

Although sales were at their peak in 2004 when over 17 million vehicles were sold, foot traffic (i.e., non-Internet customers) continued to decline. And the decline continues unabated today.

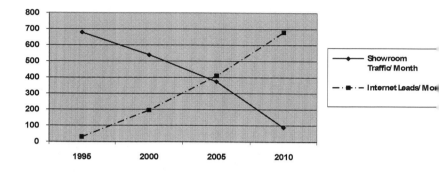

Now you're probably thinking of a myriad of excuses and explanations about how to explain the data. Perhaps you'll try to explain it away by saying "back in the day" there were fewer Dealerships, customers were looser with a dollar, financing was cheap or some combination of the above. But these various and sundry explanations fail the "Occam's razor" test which postulates – the simplest explanation tends to be the best.

Let me illustrate. In *SuperFreakonomics*, Steven Levitt and Stephen Dubner looked at our declining U.S. high school math, science, and verbal test scores to understand why the U.S. has dropped out of the Top 20 Industrialized Countries. They wondered if it was some combination of low education spending per student, poor fundamental skills, lack of parental involvement, perhaps a recent influx of non-English speaking students. No, Levitt and Dubner found out the decline in test scores was due to the Feminist movement. Huh?

48

Yes. Up until the 1970's, college educated women were largely limited to being nurses, secretaries or school teachers. But the feminist movement (Remember Helen Reddy's "I Am Woman Hear Me Roar"?) gave them new opportunities. So they entered business in unprecedented numbers which caused a massive "brain drain" in our public school system.

The "best and the brightest" women were no longer leading classrooms and encouraging more kids to attend college. Instead, they were leading business teams and encouraging more profits to fall to the bottom line. Businesses became stronger and schools became weaker.

This one explanation fulfills the "Occam's razor" test because the radical change in the quality of teachers had more impact than all other explanations combined.

So what's this got to do with your Dealership? Well, Occam's razor postulates *that the simplest explanation for the decrease in walk-in traffic is that customers don't want to talk to you!* They want to conduct business online utilizing your E-Commerce infrastructure. And can you blame them?

Customers' buying process has completely changed. Customers have already done their product research online. They have narrowed their selection to a few alternatives. They may have even configured their vehicle with exactly what they want to buy. (Just like

customers configure their computers at Dell, Apple, and HP with exactly what they want to buy.) And they know the price they are willing to pay down to the penny.

So when a customer comes to the Dealership, it's merely to evaluate the physical aesthetics they've seen online and to experience how the vehicle performs on the road. These are the only two activities that are impossible to do online.

Yet, the Dealership visit wastes customers' time with a convoluted sales process, makes customers feel ignorant about how a car works mechanically, and utilizes sales "methods of control" so customers feel manipulated. Customers come into the Dealership seeking to build an emotional bond between car and driver and instead experience agitation and aggravation.

Here's what the data tells us.

- ➤ 90+% of car buyers use the Internet as their primary information source

- ➤ Three-fourths of car buyers make their initial Dealership contact through email

- ➤ 60+% of car buyers said that if they received a competitive price and compelling reason to buy from a Dealership that they would stop shopping elsewhere

- ➤ 28% of car buyers said that if they received a competitive price and compelling reason to buy from a Dealership that they would merely compare price with one other source to ensure it was "fair and reasonable"

Now let's look at that chart of Dealership Showroom foot traffic
again. This time let's focus on the relationship between foot traffic
and internet traffic. The slope of each line is virtually the same,
although in opposite directions. This means that there has been
almost a direct substitution from Showroom Traffic to Internet Lead
traffic. Which begs the question – has your Dealership completely
transformed to address this new reality?

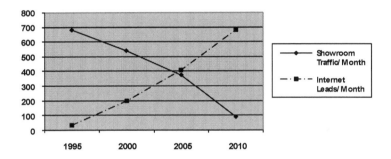

Today, most customers are willing to pay a competitive price over the
lowest price in exchange for a positive buying experience. The
Dealerships that foster a welcoming and respectful sales environment
online where the customer is treated as an individual with unique
needs tend to make higher gross profits. More important, *these
Dealerships recognize that transparency is critical – on product,
promotion, and price.*

Look no further than eBay Motors to see how well transparency sells.
eBay Motors sells one vehicle every 43 seconds by utilizing multiple
photos, vehicle specifications, descriptions, buyer feedback, and a
secure payment infrastructure. More important, all of this transparent

content is delivered in the comfort of the car buyer's home and never requires the buyer to step foot into a Dealership.

So customers are choosing with their feet to stay away and unless you adapt to the E-Commerce game, they are going to continue to stay away.

Price Transparency

One of the biggest concerns about conducting business on the Internet revolves around price transparency. Let's talk about it. There are two pricing schools of thought – "No Haggle" and "No Way."

The "No Haggle" school of thought believes that unless a price is given to the customer then the Dealership is going to be eliminated from consideration. The "No Way" school of thought believes that providing a price gives the customer the ability to "shop you."

But the real question is does it matter to customers? And if it does matter to them, what is the best course to pursue that meets their price transparency needs?

Customers tell us price transparency matters very, very much.
Customers' fundamental needs today (and we'll work on changing their needs later in the book) are centered on product availability and price. In other words, what do you have to sell me? And what will you sell it to me for?

Customers also tell us that they don't mind if the Dealership makes a profit. Some customers actually report that they want the Dealership to make a profit. These same customers also want to make sure they are getting the lowest price.

How do you reconcile these two attitudes? The long answer is that you haven't created a compelling value proposition to get customers to pay more. (See Chapters 4-6). The short answer is that there is a very easy way to present price in a way that customers perceive pricing is both "fair to the Dealership" and "a good buy."

Dan Ariely, in The New York Times non-fiction best-seller, *Predictably Irrational – The Hidden Forces That Shape Our Decisions*, conducted reams of research and discovered customers are predictably irrational when it comes to price. For instance, we all know women who've returned from shopping and shown off their latest purchase exclaiming, "Look what I got. It was 40% off!"

But when you look further at the actual purchase, you find out that

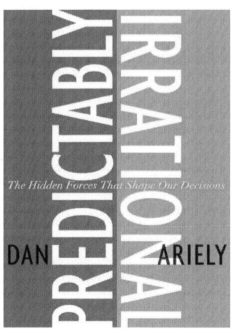

your enthusiastic lady friend paid $200 for a simple black cotton sweater. It's an outrageous amount to pay, but she used the retail price, known as an "anchor price," to determine that she was getting a "good deal."

Now, this anchor price is a manufacturer suggested retail price (MSRP). And like most MSRP's, it's a completely artificial price point. Nonetheless, the buyer "irrationally" perceives value in her purchase. And most buyers do the same thing which makes the buying behavior "predictable."

So the ideal way for Dealerships to present price to customers follows this simple format:

MSRP:	$26,985
Internet Price:	$24,350
You Save:	10%
You Save:	$2,535
Estimated Monthly Payment:	$230

There are additional guidelines from this research about the how to (and how not to) set your prices. For instance, there is a minimum amount you must discount, but if you discount too much then customers perceive, "There must be something wrong with the car."

This is completely irrational because it doesn't account for floor costs, Dealership incentives, competitive pricing, and a host of other reasons to "move the metal." But make no mistake about it, this is a real phenomenon and a quick check of any online retailer from Office Depot to JC Penny will validate this approach.

The "No Way" folks are crazy to ignore these demands, especially in light of what happened in 2004-2005 when manufacturers decided to release invoice pricing to online publishers like AutoTrader.com, Cars.com, Edmunds.com, and scores of other websites.

Customers routinely use these references to find out invoice prices. In fact, if you want to pay $39.95, James Bragg will provide you with 50+ pages of the latest pricing promotions and how to wring out every last penny of the deal.

Bragg states that only a fool would walk into a car dealership to negotiate price since new cars are just expensive commodities – the same vehicle with the same price structure at every dealership. He advocates "Email Attacks" to solicit competitive price proposals from several Dealerships. But Bragg says, "Never ever walk into a Dealership without the price locked up."

Bragg has built a multi-million dollar business providing these same words of wisdom to hundreds of thousands of customers. So go ahead "No Way" Dealerships and hold back on price if you insist. Just recognize the Dealerships around you are getting into customers' consideration set because these Dealerships have chosen to meet the customers' need for price transparency.

So may the best Dealership win. I'll put my money on the customer-centric Dealership with price transparency every time.

Exercise:

How many Internet Deals have you lost in the last month?

	Example Dealership:	Your Dealership:
Total New Internet Leads	400	
Subtract: Internet Leads Still Active	80	_____
Subtract: Internet Leads Sold	40	_____
Internet Leads "Blown Through"	280	_____
		_____

3

CHANGE IS CERTAIN. SURVIVAL IS NOT.

Getting people to think realistically about tomorrow is hard. The present is full of the "tyranny of the urgent, but unimportant." And dreaming about the future is fun. But actually getting down to dealing with the nitty-gritty reality that tomorrow is going to bring is tough.

But the Automotive Industry has amply demonstrated in recent years that if you don't plan and push forward to grab hold of tomorrow, then when it arrives you will be unprepared. Look no further than General Motors, Isuzu, Chrysler, and even Toyota for examples of being unprepared to survive and thrive tomorrow.

> ➢ GM files bankruptcy
> ➢ Chrysler files bankruptcy
> ➢ Isuzu exits North American market
> ➢ Toyota loses $5.5 Billion

So what's happening to your Dealership in the market today is a direct reflection on how well you prepared yesterday, or last month, or last year. Nothing is a sudden change. There are always signs that there is change on the horizon.

Even in the horrific tragedy of 9/11, there were many signs detected by F.B.I. agent, John O'Neill, that both a terrorist attack would occur and that it would take place at the World Trade Center. The New York Times best-seller *The Looming Tower* by Lawrence Wright, lays out all information that was known and ignored.

And things are going to change. But because change is scary, a lot of Dealerships prefer not to deal with it. "Well, let's wait and see what happens," they'll say. Or, "Who else is doing what you're suggesting?"

I understand the reasoning that if you wait for more exact qualified information, you'll reduce the risk of doing something that might not work as well as advertised. Unfortunately, it also means that if you need a laundry list of qualified references, you'll be left in the dust.

Ironically, while no Dealership wants to be left behind, no Dealership wants to go first. Yet, Einstein said, *"Doing the same thing over and over again and expecting different results is insanity."*

You need to trust yourself when you see an opportunity. Because things are going to change tomorrow. That's why change is certain. Survival is not.

Create The Future

Think about how Starbucks changed the market for coffee by redefining its uses and experiences. When you think about the future of E-Commerce in your Dealership, you have to think about ways that you can fundamentally change it to your advantage.

This is particularly important, because by defining and redefining yourself online, you can constantly move away from your direct competitors. Every time you change the definition of yourself, you put your competitors by comparison in a totally (and hopefully worse) position.

What I'm suggesting is to simply try new ways of thinking. I once took a post-graduate class at Northwestern University on Creative Thinking. (No, you didn't drink beer and stare at a fluorescent Elvis Presley. Not that there's anything wrong with that.)

In this class, the professor suggested that most of us don't know what

 we want, but that _we definitely know what we don't want_. For example, think about getting a new job. Most people struggle articulating what they would be interested in doing.

But if you ask these same people if they know what they don't want to do, then you'll get an earful. "I don't want to work for a large

corporation." "I don't want to do the same thing every day." "I don't want to just get a 1-2% raise every year." "I don't want to be far removed from solving the customer's problems."

Ok. Now just reverse the thinking to what the person does want to do. Sounds like the person in this example wants to work for a small company that's growing and where compensation is tied to performing different duties in the service of the customer. In short, an independent commissioned salesperson like an Insurance Agent.

So let's use this same process to improve your Dealerships response to Internet Leads. What do you want to make sure doesn't happen?

- Don't ignore any Internet Lead
- Don't respond later than 15 minutes
- Don't respond with a "generic" reply
- Don't leave out any product information
- Don't hide the price
- Don't limit product availability
- Don't make it hard for the Lead to ask questions
- Don't make it confusing about who to contact
- Don't fail to make a good first impression
- Don't forget to follow up with relevant content
- Etc., etc., etc.

If you change all of these (and I'm sure you can come up with more "don't" statements) to positive statements, then you will have decided what you want your E-Commerce future to be. These statements now become the technology requirements for your E-Commerce business and you can evaluate software against these requirements.

You will no longer be fooled by "bright, shiny objects" posing as technology "silver bullets." And when you begin to build the foundations of your E-Commerce businesses, you will have repositioned your Dealership. You will have put your competitors on the defensive. You will have created the future.

Why Not?

Just as the "Define What You Don't Want" exercise created a concrete outcome that your Dealership can use to define the requirements of your E-Commerce businesses, there is another technique that can create a useful service that doesn't yet exist. It's called "Why Not?"

Think about the problem that customers rarely answer the phone when the Dealership calls. Salespeople are often forced to leave multiple messages over multiple weeks and they may never get a response. But the salesperson has to diligently spend time entering all of the calls into the Dealership CRM so they can track and report their failure to connect with customers.

How much time and money does this cost? How much wear and tear does it do to the salesperson? How does this low morale adversely affect everyone around them? What if you could invent something that would flip the process?

For instance, think about a 900 phone number. When you call a 900 number, you trigger _a charge_ to your credit card. But what if you flipped the process? What if when you called the 900 number, you trigger *a payment* to your credit card.

Think about it. Instead of avoiding your Dealership's calls, customers would welcome them because they'll get paid to talk to you. You could even pay them more for spending more time with you. Instead of hanging up, customers would now say, "Are you sure there aren't any more questions?"

Or what if you paid customers when you sent an email? In the past, you paid to broadcast advertising so why not flip the process and pay for customers paying attention to you. For example, you could pay customers a dollar to open your email, pay another dollar to watch a two-minute video on the vehicle of their choice, pay another dollar to answer a survey, pay another dollar to fill out a credit application, and pay another dollar to configure the car they want to buy.

In this example, you would have spent $5 to know everything you need to know to qualify the customer as a credit worthy prospect. By thinking creatively, you solved the problem of customer indifference while providing immediate gratification to both buyer and seller. Buckle your seat belt, you're just the beginning to survive and thrive in the E-Commerce world!

Exercise:

List all of the things you want to make sure _don't_ happen when your Dealership works with Internet Leads. List everything that comes to your mind.

1.

2.

3.

4.

5.

6.

7.

8.

9.

10.

11.

12.

PART 2

SELL MORE TO MORE FOR MORE

4

WITHOUT STRATEGY YOU WON'T SURVIVE.

Strategy is everything.

Think about it: if Marketing is a business discipline, focused on selling more to more for more, it cannot be a random collection of activities. Rather, it must be a systematic planning and development of processes that succeed in convincing people to buy what you want to sell.

That doesn't mean that the tactics always have to work. Sometimes they won't. But that doesn't mean that your strategy is wrong. You may have a brilliant strategy, but may need more resources of time, people, or money.

Let's start with some clear definitions.

Objective: What you want to accomplish

Strategy: How you'll achieve your objective

Tactics: Tasks you physically do

Imagine that you are General Patton in World War II. You are in command of the Western Task Force of the U.S. Army. You are in charge of Operation Torch for the North African Campaign. You will land in Morocco, secure the port and engage the entrenched German Tank Divisions led by the cagey Desert Fox, Erwin Rommel.

Here's what Patton's strategy might look like:

Objective: (What?)	Push 10 German Panzer Divisions back 500 miles to Cairo destroying 50% of their tanks by November 6, 1942.
Strategy: (How?)	Conduct flanking maneuvers that force the German Panzer Divisions to shift from being fanned out across North Africa into a concentrated formation.
Tactics: (Physical Tasks)	Move 200 miles a day Head south to draw out enemy Attack at dawn from East Reposition during afternoon sand storms

Notice some of the characteristics of this strategic framework. First, his objective is a S.M.A.R.T. one. S.M.A.R.T. is an acronym for Specific, Measurable, Action Oriented, Realistic, and Time-bound. For General Patton, his objective is to: Push 10 German Panzer

Divisions (Specific) back 500 miles to Cairo (Measurable) destroying (Action Oriented) 50% of their tanks (Realistic) by November 6, 1942 (Time-bound).

Second, his strategy is everything. He decided to pinch and pick at

the outer flanks of the German Army. Now, he could have chosen aerial strategy using aircraft launched from carriers in the Mediterranean. Or he could have decided to attack with concentrated forces at the middle of the German position and split the enemy into two smaller groups. Or he could have moved his forces to the south and driven the German Afrika Korps north to the sea.

Why did he choose this strategy? Well, because General Patton knew that the first tanks the U.S. used to fight in World War II were fast, but their guns lacked the range of the German guns. What's more, the U.S. tanks had inadequate armor to absorb artillery hits from the German tanks. So with limited range and power, he had to hit and move – faster than the Germans could react.

Once the strategy was determined, the tactics came rather easily. That doesn't mean they were easy to execute. But they were easy to figure out. The objective was clear from the high command to the lowliest private. But it was the "Hit and Move" strategy that dictated every tactic from resupplying ammo to advancing gasoline miles in front of the attack to setting up temporary aid and mess stations.

"Hit and Move" meant something to everybody. And everyone performed better when they knew exactly "How" they were going to achieve their objective. That's why strategy is everything. And for General Patton and his troops, it was simply – Adapt. Or Die.

Why Strategy Matters

But strategy goes beyond military battles. Every business must have some strategy framework for getting work done. A strategic framework allows you to use your creativity and the creativity of your people and your vendors to chart a course for all to follow. (Yes, your vendors can and should be involved as Subject Matter Expert (SME) partners. See Chapter 7.) In the end, a clear strategy becomes a rallying point for everyone.

The power of a clear strategy cannot be underestimated. For decades, Coca-Cola rallied 50,000 employees in 100+ countries around one single strategy: Put Coca-Cola within an arm's length of desire. Everyone knew what this meant – build product availability.

So Coca-Cola folks extended their distribution from drug store fountain counters to grocery stores,

movie theaters, barber shops, diners, hardware stores, churches, county fairs, and anywhere people gathered together. The idea was that no thirst should go unquenched and this strategy built the most recognized brand in the world.

Ok, so you aren't a behemoth like The Coca-Cola Company. That doesn't matter. Everything you do, every promotion, every piece of advertising, every single activity that affects customers – which is basically everything a Dealership does – should come out and drive the strategy ahead.

And everybody who does anything that affects customers- which is basically everybody in the Dealership- needs to know what the strategy is so that he or she can make decisions and take actions that will move you ever closer to your goal or destination.

There are thousands of stories about how Dealerships were able to get short term sales spikes by running one promotion or finance offer or ad blitz. The sad fact is that none of these activities had any staying power. The reason they didn't have any staying power was because they had no strategy. They didn't communicate the essential essence of your Dealership so there were no referrals, no transference of goodwill from sales to service, no repeat customers, no interest in anything more than a one-time transaction.

Tactics In Search Of A Strategy

Go to NADA or attend a Digital Dealer Conference or any other automotive industry trade meeting. You will be overwhelmed with information, seminars, training, and sell sheets about one thing or another. Everyone is fighting for your attention and you'll do

everything possible to
avoid eye contact as you
wade through oceans of
tactical options.

Sit outside NADA and
watch what happens
outside the Exhibitor Halls.
You'll see scores of
Dealers, GM's, and Internet
Managers thumbing
through the Exhibitor Listing. They are plotting an approach to
navigate through the sea of vendors.

Consciously or unconsciously, they are determining what resources
they might need to achieve their business objectives. What they are
really doing is formulating their business strategy. On a bench. By
themselves. In usually less than 10 minutes!

But this happens every day as well. If you monitor one of the popular
Dealer, GM, Internet Manager social media websites, you'll see
immediately that the discussions all center on tactics, vendors, or
recalcitrant customers.

The tactical questions might be, "Is anyone using…?"

- Actual New Vehicle Pictures
- Trade Appraisal Tools
- BDC Tracking Scoreboards
- Phone Call Worksheets
- Parts and Service E-Commerce
- "Greenie" Training Workbooks

The vendor questions usually take the innocuous form, "What do you think of...?"

- Car GiGi
- Google Wave
- eBay Motors Templates
- AutoTrader.com Alpha
- Cars Direct

But, ultimately, the questions will evolve to address the fact that the tactics aren't working and the question become, "How do you handle...?"

- Non-responsive customers
- Customers refusing to come on the lot
- Price or "only the best price" customers
- Customer that NEVER call or email

Guess what? This particular automotive industry networking site averages over 500 discussions per month and after viewing thousands of discussions and postings, *there was not one reference to strategy!*

Yet, there is plenty of this kind of dialog:

Internet Manager #1:

I have to blow off some steam. I just got off the phone with 2 customers in a row that never responded to one email, never returned one phone call...no response at all...until they purchased something else. When I asked them if they received my emails, phone calls, and price quotes, they said, "Oh, yeah, we got them." Why is this happening?

Internet Manager #2:

I feel your pain. It happens to me all the time. It's a numbers game. You're going to fail 90% of the time.

Internet Manager #3:

I have to chime in here because I had THREE yesterday that were identical to what you are saying! I feel that I am very creative in how I contact people, send information, make phone calls...etc. It is very irritating.

Internet Manager #4:

But there has to be something we can do better to elicit a response from these people. It does feel like I missing something in the communication process. WHAT ARE WE MISSING?

These poor folks are working so hard on all the wrong things. You can tell because:

> Tactics aren't strategically connected

> Tactics lack specific performance requirements

> Tactics supposedly work for every Dealership

These comments show how frustrating it is to execute tactics with no strategic reason for doing it. The result is that they are frustrated and nervous that they'll lose their jobs. It's hard not to feel bad for them. They are working diligently on *tactics in search of a strategy*.

Strategic Sacrifice

Now you might be thinking that if I narrow my focus then I won't appeal to everybody. That's exactly the point. Every good strategy means you make sacrifices. And when you don't, then you have no shot at creating a sustainable advantage.

Supermarkets are the perfect example of trying to be all things to all people. They operate with no strategy at all. They merely open close to densely populated residential locations and count on the fact that people will get hungry and need food.

Food manufacturers support this lunacy by creating products for clerks to stack on a shelf, sending a point-of-sale piece, and then hoping somebody buys. Yes, they hope that their stuff sells because they manufactured it, delivered it, and discount priced it. But what about marketing? What about analyzing customers and communicating something that connects with them?

Supermarkets aren't the only businesses that operate without a clear strategy. Michael Treacy and Fred Wiersema give more examples in *"The Discipline of Market Leaders."*

> ➤ Why is it that it only takes a few minutes and no paperwork to pick up or drop off a rental car at Hertz's #1 Club Gold, but twice that time and an annoying process to check into a Hilton hotel? Are they afraid you'll steal the room?

> Why is it that FedEx can "absolutely, positively" deliver a package overnight, but Delta, American, and United Airlines have trouble delivering your bags on the same plane you're riding on? Do they think you don't care?

> Why is it that Lands' End remembers your last order and family member's sizes, but after 10 years as an American Express card holder, you are still being solicited to join? Don't they know you're already a customer?

To survive in today's marketplace, you must understand the battle in which you're engaged. You cannot be all things to all people or you will be nothing to everybody. *You must define your value by raising customer expectations in the one component of value that's important to customers.*

Wal-Mart, for instance, provides "always lower prices", but they don't try to peddle haute couture. Their game is high volume, low margin and consequently they strip out cost everywhere along the supply chain. But that doesn't mean they strip cost out everywhere. They

still aggressively invest in technology that makes their supply chain run like a Swiss watch. Because that's important to Wal-Mart's core business strategy.

On the other hand, Starbucks charges more for a cup of coffee than anyone else. But

Starbucks doesn't try to slide a cup of java under your nose faster or more conveniently than anyone else. They differentiate their product offerings with weekly flavors, seasonal limited time tastes, and even hundreds of ways to customize coffee the way you want it.

And Lands' End doesn't sell clothing for the lowest cost. Nor does it sell a stitch of what could be considered "fashion." But Lands' End knows everything you've ever ordered and keeps track of your sizes (and knows just as well as your spouse that you've been putting on weight). This knowledge allows them to make helpful suggestions and produce targeted catalogs designed specifically for you. They have honed the one component of value to a level of excellence that crushes their competition.

Each one of these companies sacrificed something to be the best at something else. By declaring what they do well, customers learn to trust and depend on them. Customers become loyal to the familiar predictable experience. And because customers know what they are and what they aren't, it's easy for them to refer other customers to enjoy the experience.

These companies consciously sacrificed to make one component of value the focal point of everything they do. And based on their tremendous sales and profitability clearly demonstrate that their strategic sacrifice was not made in vain.

Exercise:

Write one S.M.A.R.T. business objective for your Dealership. For example, "We will generate 3,000 Unique Visitors to our website creating 300 Internet Leads that will result in 150 new and pre-owned vehicles sold with an average gross of $1500/vehicle each month."

Specific: _____

Measurable: _____

Action Oriented: _____

Realistic: _____

Time-bound: _____

5

STEAL THE BEST AND LEAVE THE REST

Eleanor Roosevelt once said, "Learn from the mistakes of others. You won't live long enough to make all the mistakes on your own." She was right but Dealerships have embraced this thinking for all the wrong reasons. Dealerships seek to avoid mistakes like all good businesses. That's why 20 Groups exist and informal Dealership networks exist everywhere.

But as Chapter 4 points out, Dealers, GM's and Internet Managers collaborate about tactics and ignore core operating strategies. Before ever assigning any person to execute a tactic, the key question for the Dealership to ask should be, "Why should we do this?" The follow-up question should be, "Is this important to create customer demand?" And the final question should be, "What do we specifically expect from this effort?"

What's Your Strategy?

To illustrate how a potential strategy discussion can quickly erode to disjointed tactics, I've selected a blog from a Dealer Principal and some of the reactions generated by other Dealers, GM's, and Internet Managers. There were over 100 replies so I chose the few that best summarized different trains of thought. (Comments in *italics* are mine.)

> "I think the reason Dealership websites are such a conundrum, and, therefore, the reason we Dealers devote great amounts of money to SEO management vendors, 3rd party lead providers, talking website avatars and industry best practices seminars, is because we don't understand what we want our websites to do for us." *(Great! The Dealer recognizes the need to establish S.M.A.R.T. objectives.)*

> "Nor do we know how to get our websites to do what we need to get done. *(Excellent! Now we're going to discuss strategy – How To Achieve S.M.A.R.T. objectives.)*

> "But in the end, isn't all retail just a matter of luck? *(Luck?! No, it's BIG M Marketing.)*

> "Isn't that especially true in automotive retailing? How many of us held a big sale and no one showed up. How many of us have had a temporary sales surge for which we have no explanation?" *(Hold on. Just because you don't know the answer, doesn't mean there wasn't one.)*

"So since nobody knows nothing, I looked at a bunch of good Dealership websites and came up with a formula that's sure to work for everyone." *(Wait, if "nobody knows nothing," how can there be a formula?)*

This blog concluded by asking for input from others. And in the absence of any strategy, a group of 22 Dealers, GM's, and Internet Managers fell headlong into the "tactics trap."

Here's what they determined was important:

1. Bright, engaging color scheme
2. Readily available live chat
3. Easy to find inventory
4. Photos of the actual vehicles (new and used)
5. Online credit application
6. "About Us" with staff photos and mission statement
7. Online service scheduler
8. Video walk-around of all vehicles
9. "Wish List" to "park" a car and come back later
10. "My Account" feature
11. Ability to sort vehicles by estimated payment
12. Lifetime Car Washes
13. Lifetime Inspections
14. Free Birthday Oil Change
15. Annual Holiday eCard

If this is the approach taken, then the blog author is probably correct that his sales are random acts of luck. However, a disciplined Marketing strategy will yield consistent results over time. Any Marketing initiative can be debriefed and reconciled to know exactly what did

work and what didn't work and why.

We'll go back to these tactics later and see where and how they might fit with a well defined strategy. To be clear, these tactics aren't inherently "bad," just not strategically linked.

Three Strategy Choices

So what are the best strategies to survive in this customer controlled environment? How do these strategies work? What can be learned from other industries and businesses so your Dealership doesn't make all the mistakes on your own?

According to Michael Treacy and Fred Wiersema in, *The Discipline Of Market Leaders*, there are only three strategies for you to consider. And each strategy demands different operating processes. Most important, the choice you make establishes the inner workings of the Dealership from acquiring customers to delivery to service.

Fortunately, you don't have to labor and deliberate over which strategy to choose. Customers have effectively already made your strategic choice for you. Remember, customers are in control. You lost your leverage when customers gained "perfect information" and "price transparency." So the good news is you don't have to worry about which strategy to adopt and can focus all of your efforts on how to execute that strategy with distinction.

The three strategies are:

1. Product Differentiation
2. Customer Intimacy
3. Operational Excellence

Product Differentiation

A Dealership pursuing product differentiation needs an inventory of products that push the envelope. Their manufacturers must concentrate on offering vehicles that expand performance boundaries or can reasonably claim to be uniquely designed for unusual experiences.

Dealerships benefit from a manufacturer that consistently challenges itself to be creative. More than anything else, being creative means recognizing and embracing ideas that will set a new standard. However, in the automotive industry, the problem with true product innovation is the tremendous risk involved. Design is difficult and manufacturing production costs are sky high. So while a hit product has a huge payoff, a failed innovation can break the bank.

Consequently, product differentiation often comes in a blend of experiential advertising and product personality. By definition, these products tend to appeal to small but loyal customer segments that drive the vehicle as a reflection of their own unique personality.

However, the product attributes must mesh with the personality traits. For instance, Saturn tried to create a "cult of personality" among its customers, but the product itself was bland and undistinguishable so belonging to this "cult" said very little about the owner. There was no "reason to believe" Saturn's claims. Soon Saturn owners became less and less interested in participating in Saturn owner events.

The only brand to receive
Motor Trend's Sport/Utility of the Year
two years in a row. Read More ▸
The All-New 2010 Outback.
Motor Trend's 2010 Sport/Utility of the Year.

In contrast, Land Rover uses its heritage as an off-road vehicle to project a personality of rugged individualism. So while Saturn failed to mesh with its projected personality, Land Rover meshes seamlessly. And we all know what happened to Saturn.

Here are the few remaining vehicle brands that can credibly execute a Product Differentiation strategy.

- Jeep
- Land Rover
- Subaru
- Volkswagen

Customer Intimacy

A Dealership that delivers value via customer intimacy builds bonds with customers like those between good neighbors. Customer intimate Dealerships make a business of knowing the people it sells to and the products and services they need.

For instance, BMW offers a Teen Driving School tailoring its products and services so it can credibly claim, "We take care of you and all your needs. We get you the best total solution." The customer-intimate Dealership's greatest asset is, not surprisingly, its customer loyalty and word of mouth referrals.

Customer-intimate Dealerships don't advertise or price promote. Customer-intimate companies don't try to pursue transactions; they cultivate relationships. They are adept at giving the customer more than he or she expects. By constantly upgrading their offerings, customer-intimate companies stay ahead of their customers' rising expectations.

To move quickly in responding to customers, these Dealerships maintain state-of-the-art software capabilities to track and monitor all of the activities and interactions with a given customer. For this knowledge, the Dealership is rewarded with greater customer retention, higher fixed operations visits, and less price sensitivity.

Customer-intimate Dealerships tend to sell vehicles from "high-line" manufacturers.

- Bentley
- BMW
- Cadillac
- Jaguar
- Lamborghini
- Lexus
- Mercedes Benz
- Porche

Operational Excellence

Operationally excellent Dealerships deliver a combination of quality, price, and ease of purchase. They are not innovators, nor do they cultivate one-to-one relationships with their customers. They execute extraordinarily well, and their value proposition to customers is low price and hassle-free service.

Operationally excellent Dealerships recognize that selling is nothing more than a transaction that must be executed efficiently and inexpensively. Consequently, these Dealerships are characterized with processes for end-to-end sales and service transactions that are optimized to minimize cost and hassle. Operations are standardized, simplified, and tightly controlled, focusing on integrated, reliable, high-speed transactions that result in high inventory turnover.

Customers have forced the majority of Dealerships to accept this strategy. Rightly or wrongly, customers perceive little product differentiation today so they seek the Dealership that demonstrates operational excellence above all else.

Gone are the days where relationships and handshakes could result in a sale at these Dealerships. For one thing, how can you have a relationship when turnover is so high at the Dealership? Who is the customer supposed to connect with? The Dealer is usually off-site or in an office and the GM is sequestered behind glass at "The Desk."

Nissan is beginning to recognize this need to shift to a hassle-free transaction. Note the headline, "A to Z" reinforced with the sub-headline, "Quality, Reliability, Value." These are core value propositions for company striving to be operationally excellent.

Here are the other Brands from whom customers seek Operational Excellence:

- Acura
- Buick/GMC
- Chevrolet
- Chrysler
- Dodge
- Ford
- Honda
- Hyundai
- Infiniti
- Lincoln Mercury
- Mazda
- Mitsubishi
- Nissan
- Toyota
- Volvo

Strategic Choice and Marriage

So now you know which strategy customers demand from your Dealership. What does your strategic choice have to do with marriage? I could write an entire other book (or series of books) on that topic. Suffice it to say that once you decide on your strategy, you must remain loyal and true.

You can't decide on a strategy and change it in a few months. That's the equivalent of getting married and divorced in a few months. It's expensive. It's painful. And it's going to cost you a lot more than you can ever imagine.

And just like marriage, the first few months are going to be both exciting and frustrating. You'll be unsure about a lot of decisions. You'll have to say goodbye to a lot of things (and people) that have made you comfortable. You'll doubt whether you can make it through or whether it's worth it. And just like marriage you'll often look longing backward and wish things were liked they used to be.

Well, get over it. The image you hold in your head about your Dealership and reality are two different things. It's a trap we all get into everyday. You may search Facebook to find that cute girl you knew in high school twenty years ago because you're certain she's just as attractive today as she was when you used to dream about her. That image remains in your mind until you find her Facebook page, look at her picture, and you feel like you got hit by a 2 x 4.

You cannot go back to the good old days. You cannot rely on your rolodex of old customers to build new sales. You cannot blitz the airwaves about a "party" you're throwing at the Dealership and expect

armies of people to show up. You must face reality. Choose a single strategy. And commit for the long haul.

So how do you keep your strategic marriage fresh and exciting? Remember the Coca-Cola example of putting Coca-Cola within an arm's length reach of desire. That strategy is decades old and still gets refreshed every day. How does it get refreshed? With new communication messages, new promotional events, new product launches, new PR announcements. Every tactical activity makes the marriage fresh, new, exciting.

This happens in a marriage as well. It gets refreshed with new communication messages (i.e., birthday cards and gifts), new promotional events (i.e., vacations), new product launches (i.e., kids), new PR announcements (i.e., 40th Birthday, 20th Anniversary).

And just because the surprise birthday party you gave to your wife didn't go over so well, that doesn't mean you give up on your marriage. You have to keep trying new and different tactics, but don't change your strategy. It's far easier to adapt with new tactics than to die a slow death changing strategies.

Not choosing means ending up in a muddle. It means hybrid operating models that are neither here nor there, and that indecision recreates confusion, tension, and loss of energy. It means there's no clear way to resolve conflicts or set priorities. It means high turnover and high training costs. Not choosing means creating managerial complexity that results in doing business with yourself internally, rather than with your customers.

Take comfort in the successes of others that have gone on before you. And learn from their mistakes so that you might live to fight another day.

Exercise:

List all of your Dealership's sales tactics. Then for each tactic select the strategy that fits best. Finally, compare the strategy you are following today with the strategy customers think you should follow.

Your Dealership's Current Sales Tactics	Product Differentiation	Customer Intimacy	Operational Excellence
Direct Mail Newsletters	☐	☐	☐
Price Promotion Email	☐	☐	☐
_____	☐	☐	☐
_____	☐	☐	☐
_____	☐	☐	☐
_____	☐	☐	☐
_____	☐	☐	☐
_____	☐	☐	☐

6

WHAT DOES SUCCESS LOOK LIKE?

Now let's take a look at each strategy in more detail so you can understand more fully what success would look like for your Dealership. It's often easier to explain these strategies when you see how other companies execute in the real world. This chapter will be peppered with examples to ground your thinking.

If you aren't familiar with the examples offered here, I encourage you to go on a "market visit" to experience first-hand how these stores operate. There is a belief among Dealers, GM's, and Internet Managers that the car business is "different." Well, if I had a dime for every time I've heard that from people in other industries, I'd be sipping margaritas on a beach in Barbados.

The auto industry is more similar to every other industry than it is different. There are customers to attract. There are needs to be met.

There is competition to defeat. There is an exchange of money. There is delivery of the product or service.

These are the elements to focus on. And each strategy must deal with them. But they will do it differently and those are the differences to focus on.

Product Differentiation

This strategy is the hardest to execute, especially since so much is out of the control of the Dealership. Because what wakes customers up is product innovation – products that deliver real benefit and performance improvements that cannot be found anywhere else.

This is hard work. Customers aren't impressed by one-time innovations followed by countless "improvements." Customers look for a steady stream of standout products and services that turn people's heads and make their hearts beat faster.

Apple introduced the online Apple Store, the iPod, iTunes, iMac, and the iPhone in less than 10 years. Apple change how people buy customer electronics, how they listen to music, how they work, and

how they communicate. In the process of continually reinventing itself, Apple destroyed independent computer, CD, and phone retailers. They took power away from entertainment moguls and even wrestled it away from the powerful telecom behemoths.

Nike products indulge people's hunger for association with sports heroes, the rich and famous, or peer recognition. Nike knows that it's the experience and the emotional impact that matters. That's why the Nike tagline, "Just Do It" has become part of the American lexicon. It connects with customers on a very personal level in the same way that Revlon sells hope, not cosmetics.

This craving for a mix of tangible and experiential benefits draws people into the store. These customers expect the performance of the products to motivate and inspire both their rational and emotional selves.

Harley-Davidson captures this spirit. Harley-Davidson has sold out of every limited edition motorcycle they have ever produced long before the first product ever rolled out of the factory. There are over 500,000 members in the Harley Owners Group, which sponsors rallies where members compete in H.O.G. games and they pay an annual fee for the privilege of membership. Each year Harley-Davidson accessories outsell motorcycles. Harley customers buy more than a motorcycle; they buy a personal statement.

Think about how VW customers personalize their car. They put flowers on the dash. Beads hang from the rear view mirror. Customized frames hold license plates that read, LUV BUG. Everything screams out "I'm Different."

And guess whose tagline is "Think Different." That's right. The king of product differentiation – Apple.

Dealership Big Idea:

So what can a Dealership do to create real product differentiation? *Authentic experiences.*

This is a "pull" strategy as opposed to a "push" strategy. The difference is significant because one puts the burden of the relationship on the customer and the other puts the burden squarely on the Dealership. In both cases, it is critical to provide rewards for participating in the relationship and to utilize relevant engaging content.

A "pull" strategy is designed to pull in customers to the relationship with the Dealership. In essence, the Dealership needs to build a community based on common interests and shared values. You will be asking people to commit their time, energies, and talents to be part of something bigger than themselves.

This participation is a personal statement about who they are and how they want others to see them. Tap into this vein of consciousness and you've tapped into the mother lode of loyalty.

Needless to say, there are some core requirements that must be met in order to pull customers into your "cult of personality." Think about what it takes to build an enduring social community and you'll understand the need to meet the following requirements to execute this strategy.

Requirements:

- Make long-term commitment of at least three (3) years
- Keep content continually refreshed; at least weekly updates

- Involve customers in contributing content
- Focus on affiliation; do not try to sell products or services

Big Idea:

Build a loyalty program exclusively for Dealership vehicle owners based on the authentic experiences they've had with their vehicle.

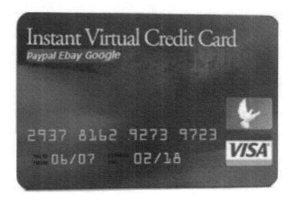

Mechanics:

- Hand out a VISA Debit loyalty card with every vehicle sale customized with the Dealership logo
- Create a "Members Only" Fixed Operations website for preferred appointments and offers
- Create a special toll-free number for preferred access to specially treatment for all your Dealership needs
- Provide incentives and contests for content contributors rewarding members with TREK bikes, Gift Certificates at REI or Pro Bass, Nike Sports Apparel
- Provide membership benefits including discounts at online retailers like Amazon, Best Buy, Sharper Image and more

Financial Details:
This is a self-funding program. Customers sign up online to register their VISA Debit Card and transfer funds to activate the card. Every transaction generates revenue from the issuing bank for the Dealership. Some of this revenue is set aside to fund ongoing customer content incentive programs and the remainder of the revenue flows to the bottom line.

What's Required From Customers?

Customers must activate the card and utilize it throughout the year to maintain membership. Each transaction generates "points" which can be deemed for Fixed Operations service, Accessories or Branded Dealership apparel.

What's Required From The Dealership?

Website content updates, email campaigns to members, incentive programs to visit Fixed Operations.

Who Can Help?

Mike Buczkowski at The Ignition Network. (312) 893-5002. mike@theignitionnetwork.com. 125 South Wacker Drive, Suite 1750, Chicago, IL 60606

Customer Intimacy

Successful customer-intimate companies are those that have become expert at understanding their customers' needs and at creating solutions. But no matter what their formula for combining help in using the product, advice on caring for the product, and responsibility for keeping it running at peak performance, these companies deploy a series of processes that capture every interaction with the customer.

Customer-intimate companies have integrated computer infrastructures that can tell you a lot about the customer – what catches the attention of each customer, what individual customers want to know more about, what motivates customers to act.

Deeply rooted in the culture of a customer-intimate company is the sense that everyone either adds or subtracts value in what they do. There is a conscious effort to be of service regardless of the request. These companies always answer, "Yes, I can do that AND…" The "AND" might be that it costs more, takes longer, or requires the customer to do something to achieve the goal.

Customer-intimate companies take the long view. Thus, the initial transaction is merely the start of the relationship. These companies are more than happy to begin the relationship with very little profit being made. They recognize that the onus is on them to convert a transaction to a steady client – a lasting asset.

Go shop at Nordstrom. A guest services person (not a salesperson) will greet you and ask "how may I serve you?" You may walk into the store to get a new pair of shoes. So while you start in the shoe department, the guest services person will anticipant your need for some socks to go with your new shoes. Not only will she suggest this as an option, she will go with you to the sock  department and select some that she believes will meet your needs. Then, she will ask if you've got a belt to match the shoes. From there, she might take you to see the new slacks that have just arrived. She fundamentally understands that men don't like to shop and need help. She got you to open your wallet and pay for the customer intimacy.

Book a vacation with Four Seasons Hotel. When you make the reservation, you'll be asked who will be staying in the room. When you arrive, your children will have their name spelled out in multi-colored sponges next to the bathtub. They'll have sunscreen, a hat, and pool toys – all carefully arranged in a sand bucket – ready for your child to head to the beach. At night, there will be personalized note to each child from the child care center letting them know about all of the fun activities scheduled for the next day. Yes, the Four Seasons Hotel charges premium prices AND they surprise you every day with complementary gifts and thoughtful suggestions.

This strategy works when the customer sees and appreciates the opportunity to continue to do business. The customer must also have limited knowledge of what you offer. And the customer must have large untapped potential.

Every law firm recognizes that a large company meets these basic criteria. There is certainly an opportunity to continue to do business since remaining in legal compliance is an on-going challenge. Of course, the law firm by definition has more expertise that the businesses that hire them. And the complex operations of a large company represent large untapped potential. So the partners of the law firm spend endless hours wining and dining the business decision makers. They make contributions to the decision makers' charity projects. They serve on boards chaired by the decision makers. They will do everything possible to become as intimate as possible so they might become a "trusted advisor."

Fortunately, it's much easier for a Lexus Dealer to gain the "trusted advisor" status. Every vehicle needs continual maintenance, but Lexus customers want to make sure their investment is operating at peak performance. These customers are not "Do-It-Yourself" (DIY) mechanics that will roll under the chassis to change the oil. They are unlikely to know where to find the battery and certainly can't diagnose a warning light. In short, they have large untapped potential long after the initial sale.

Dealership Big Idea:

So what can a Dealership do to create real customer intimacy? _Concierge Services_.

This is a "push" strategy where the burden of performance lies with the Dealership. A "push" strategy is designed to push Dealership messages to customers in order to build the relationship between the customer and the Dealership. In this case, the Dealership needs to build the relationship based on the Dealership's ability to alleviate stress for its new and pre-owned customer base.

These customers will pay a premium for you to eliminate hassles from their lives. Your "push" is not to sell products or services, but to provide services that eliminate stress and worry. Every message should answer the question, "How can we help you…"

For instance, how can we help you prepare your vehicle for summer or winter? How can we make sure your warranty stays valid? How can we help you get the most out of your vehicle? How can we help you get your disabled vehicle into the Dealership service department?

Again, there are some core requirements for executing this strategy that must be met in order to effectively push messages to your customers. With this strategy, you must communicate personally with customers on a one on one basis.

Requirements:

- Make long-term commitment of at least three (3) years
- Create one on one problem/solution messages
- Deliver messages from women, not men
- Focus on personal assistance; do not try to sell products or services
- Never involve salespeople in the process unless it's requested by the customer

Big Idea:

Launch a "Yes, we can!" 24/7 Customer Services Center

Mechanics:

- Create toll-free number, iChat, and email interaction options for concierge services
- Staff concierge center with women 35-49
- Create "Concierge Services" website for Dealership
- Build knowledge base of customer questions and Dealership replies/solutions

Financial Details:

This is a variable funded program. There is a flat fee for the training and maintenance of the services (usually $2-3k per month). However, every transaction includes a "convenience fee" equal to 10% of the services delivered.

For example, if a towing service is necessary, then a $10 convenience fee is added or 10% of the towing service expense, whichever is higher. If an after-hours Fixed Operations appointment is made, an internal charge of $10 or 10% of the service charge, whichever is higher, is made.

What's Required From Customers?
Customers must register online and provide their vehicle information (Year, Make, Model, Mileage, Month/Year Purchased).

What's Required From The Dealership?

Phone and email campaigns to owners; incentive programs to visit Fixed Operations.

Who Can Help?

Jim Bell at Aximal. (800) 423-4610. jbell@aximal.com.

Operational Excellence

Operationally excellent companies focus on multiple tangible and intangible costs. To be sure, price remains the focus of operationally excellent companies – prices so low that customers sometimes marvel "How do they do it?" These companies recognize that there is value in volume sales, fast inventory turns, and efficient operations.

When operationally excellent companies talk of low – or lowest – prices, they mean prices that are consistently low. Anybody can hold a clearance sale or President's Day promotion. Operationally excellent companies trumpet their low cost prices every day.

These companies also stress convenience – the ease of doing business. The strength of these companies lies in the delivery of swift, dependable service. Transactions are easy, pleasant, quick, and accurate. Occasional mistakes may happen, but they're so uncommon that they're remarkable.

These companies deploy efficient operating procedures that reject variety, because it burdens the business with cost. And since they cannot be all things to all people, they work at shaping customer's expectations. If price is their strong point, they provide only the basic levels of service.

Southwest airlines doesn't offer meals or reserved seating, but it lures short-haul business travelers with its frequent departure schedule and super-low prices. Southwest's value proposition is: Better than driving. Nothing more. Nothing less.

Dell let's you order your computer online with the features that are most important to you. They offer a financing arm to structure your payments, term, and warranty coverage. They will let you track your computer being built. You will receive an estimated ship date so you can even keep an eye on your computer as it's handed off to FedEx or another transportation carrier. But don't try to walk into a Dell store because there aren't any. By focusing on operational excellence, Dell became the #1 computer manufacturer in the world in less than a dozen years.

More recently, companies have found even greater efficiency through virtual integration. Today, operationally excellent companies view themselves and their vendors not as adversarial entities, but as members of a single product supply team. Streamlining the connections among team members eliminates duplications, delays, and even payment complications that come from arms-length handoffs.

These companies require their vendors to work together and simply assign a single person to be the team leader representing the company. More important, these operationally excellent companies elevated the status of their supplies from "Vendors" to Subject Matter Expert

(SME) "Partners." This is more than a semantic change. Partners are assigned the responsibility for managing the entire end to end process ensuring the smooth flow of a transaction. And Partners meet routinely to review key metrics and create brainstorm solutions to reduce costs or increase sales. This joint venture process brings forward "best practices" at no additional cost to the company.

At the core of the operationally excellent business is a robust information technology system. Fortunately, software applications known as "Software as a Service" (SaaS) and cheap computing power make information technology systems affordable for Dealerships. The systems – and related databases and applications – are so highly automated that they don't just track the process, they contain and perform it. For example, at FedEx everyone who deals with the movement of a package uses the same package bar code to coordinate the work. This tracking system is available not only to internal FedEx employees, but also is exposed to the sender and receiver of the package. True transparency.

What would happen if a Honda Dealership could track a specific customer like FedEx? Imagine knowing exactly what an online customer viewed, how often they returned to learn more, when they interacted with your virtual inventory. What if this online customer could actually navigate through a sales process like Amazon? How many more vehicles would you sell? How many more accessories and F&I products might you add? What would happen to your gross profit? And what if this same customer could be tracked through your Fixed Operations system with every online move automatically recorded. How many more Fixed Operations appointment could you set? How much would your Fixed Operations revenue grow?

What then distinguishes operational excellence from mere operational competence? Hard choices: Leadership from the top, getting the GM to own the outcome, tapping the Subject Matter Expertise of vendors, implementing new processes and technologies, and leaving behind the people that no longer make the grade.

Dealership Big Idea:

So what is required for a Dealership to create Operational Excellence? Well, this is the challenge for most Dealerships. It is not a strategy that can be as easily implemented as the Product Differentiation and Customer Intimacy strategies.

Don't misunderstand. All business model strategic shifts are gut-wrenching and require steadfast leadership from top to bottom of the organization. However, Operational Excellence is a fundamental restructuring of people and process that requires some discussion and focus on the details.

That's what Chapters 7-12 are all about.

Exercise:

Close your eyes. Imagine you are only four years old with very little patience and all the money you have in the world is tightly squeezed in your hand. What would the Dealership have to say to get you to open your hand and give all of the money to the Dealership? (Hint: Your answer will provide clues about your current strategy.)

_____

_____

_____

_____

_____

_____

_____

_____

_____

_____

_____

_____

PART 3

GET IT DONE

7

HOW TO UNLEASH YOUR TIGER TEAM

The battle for sales and profitability never ends in the automotive industry. Neither the single store Dealership, nor the multi-store groups like AutoNation or Penske, can hope for a cease-fire. Because the customer is in control, owners and managers of both small and large Dealerships lie awake at night trying to answer the same question: "How do we compete and win in our marketplace?"

It's surprising how many Dealerships struggle to answer that question. The answer should be a short, pithy phrase that's on the tip of everyone's tongue. In the hamburger world, Wendy's is "Healthier Fast Food." McDonalds is "Food, Folks, and Fun." Burger King is "Have It Your Way."

The longer the answer to the question, the less likely your Dealership knows how to compete and win. The best answer any Dealership can give is one that defines precisely how the Dealership creates value for its customers. You've reached nirvana when everyone can articulate their role in executing this strategy.

Who's A Tiger?

The good news is that every Dealership can achieve nirvana. But first you must create a Tiger Team to conduct three rounds of disciplined assessment. Tiger Teams are small groups of high performers tasked with turning strategy into practical solutions for the store.

The ideal Tiger Team should include a coalition of Dealership personnel and vendor partners with specific roles. The Dealership personnel should include the GM, Internet Manager, Finance Manager, and Fixed Operations Manager. The vendor partners should include the Dealership's Website Provider, CRM Provider, DMS Provider, and Professional Services Integrator.

There are distinct advantages in bringing in your vendor partners. First, they have Subject Matter Expertise (SME) that you don't.

Second, they have a broader perspective than you because they work with multiple Dealerships every day. Third, they bring an incredible energy born from the fact that there isn't much they won't do for a Dealership that treats them with respect.

Your Tiger Team will go through three distinct stages of growth called "Form, Norm, and Storm." All groups go through these stages as they get to know each other and begin to work as a team. Selecting the participants is the first stage or "Form."

But it's not enough to simply call these people together and order them to "figure it out and get back to me." Part of the formation of the team is to provide leadership and to remove obstacles. Below is a list of "Do's" and "Don'ts" to make sure your Tiger Team is successful.

Your Tiger Team is by definition hungry and eager. Your biggest challenge will be to direct their energies. Here's a checklist for how to motivate and inspire your Tiger Team:

- Require regular updates in person – there's no substitute for your presence and attention

- Don't hoard information – share your performance numbers to track against milestones

- Fix internal communication problems – make your expectations crystal clear

- Give access to people who know things – this includes salespeople, customers, other vendors

- Pick up the phone and say "thanks" – this will get you 10x return on your investment

Now that you've
fired up your Tiger
Team, be aware of
their eagerness to
please you. These
earnest efforts can
lead to "group
think." Every group
has them and they

can blind you from selecting the best strategy and tactics. And the
results can be disastrous. Look no further than the U.S. Bay of Pigs
fiasco where the Kennedy administration botched an invasion of
Cuba.

Do NOT:

- Underestimate competitors that look different or operate in a
  different way from you

- Select different strategies for different departments (i.e., New
  vs. Pre-Owned vs. Fixed Operations)

- Shut down ideas or discussion among the management team

- "Go along to get along" if you believe it's important to bring
  out and resolve differences

The next step in the growth and development of the Tiger Team is to
"Norm." The goal in this stage of development for the Tiger Team is
to establish a common understanding and a common language about
the current health of the Dealership.

This is important as the Tiger Team struggles with three specific issues:

1. Determine where Dealership wants to go *(S.M.A.R.T. Objectives)*

2. Figure out how to get there *(Strategy)*

3. Define what needs to be done by whom *(Tactics)*

Round 1: Where Are We Today?

In round one, the Tiger Team must come to an understanding of where the Dealership currently stands and why. Only with a shared perspective of the current situation - based on facts, not opinions - can a Dealership evaluate its performance honestly.

- What are the dimensions of value that customers care most about?

- For each dimension of value, what percentage of customers focus on it as their primary or sole decision criterion?

- Which competitive Dealerships provide the best value in each of these value dimensions?

- Where does your Dealership stand relative to its competitors along these dimensions?

- Where and why does it fall short?

Each industry has a set of customer dimensions of value specific to the industry. These are the "must do's" in order to survive.

Industry	Dimensions of Value
Quick Service Restaurants	Food Quality
	Value
	Convenience
Banks	Secure
	Accessible
	Easy To Do Business With
Hotels	Clean
	Comfortable
	Safe
Auto Dealerships	Hassle-free Buying
	Product Availability
	Fair Price

For Dealerships, hassle-free buying has three principle components: breadth and depth of pre-purchase information; purchase efficiency; speed and accuracy of in-store product delivery. Each component puts varying demands on customers' time. And each component adds or detracts from the likelihood customers will buy from your Dealership.

Product availability is critical to match customer needs with the specific vehicle of choice. With more options, come more demands. Customer technology author, Chris Anderson, described this phenomenon in his book, *The Long Tail: Why The Future Of Business*

Is Selling Less Of More – the need to stock every item under the sun on the off-chance that someone will want it. While this is impossible in a "Brick and Mortar" showroom, it's much more attainable in a "Virtual Showroom."

Price, of course, is a crucial dimension that stands as a surrogate for all of these value components. When the transaction is not hassle-free or the product is not available exactly as specified or there's no coherent strategy that builds perceptual value in the customer's mind, then the customer will extract every last nickel and dime out of the transaction.

First, your Tiger Team should rate each competitive Dealership from +5 to -5 against these core value components. Your Tiger Team should draw on its collective knowledge where your Dealership has lost business over the past year and why the business was lost. This will result in an accurate fact-based assessment.

The next step takes courage. Your Tiger Team will rate your Dealership on the same core value components. The process may reveal things that you do not want to face. You may have invested in technology or sales process that is not creating value that's meaningful to your customers. Painful as it may be, this exercise must take place before your Dealership can be strategically repositioned to compete and win.

Round 2: How To Change?

In the second round of discussions, the Tiger Team shifts from agreeing on what it is today to agreeing on how it needs to change to achieve its S.M.A.R.T objectives.

To get started, the Tiger Team should explore the following questions for each dimension of value that was discovered in Round One:

> What are the benchmarks of value performance that will affect customer's expectations?

> How do your closest competitive Dealerships achieve these standards?

> How is the operating model of these Dealerships designed to attain these levels of performance?

This is the time where all three strategic choices need to be mapped against what is most important to customers. At the end of this phase of work, the Tiger Team should have a clear understanding of what's important to customers and what is most likely to generate the most profit in the short and long term.

For example, say your Dealership sells Chevrolet vehicles. It may be difficult to implement a product differentiation strategy. While there are Corvette and Camaro lovers, what unique product features does Chevrolet offer across the entire product line that makes the Chevrolet experience unique, different and special? How likely is a Chevrolet Dealership to create a "cult" of Chevrolet loyalists? Are customers going to be willing to pay more to join this cult? Does the Chevy Cobalt or Malibu get customers' hearts racing with excitement. If not, then the Product Differentiation strategy is probably not viable.

Now, let's test the fit of a Customer Intimacy strategy with this same Chevrolet Dealership. Do Chevrolet customers want to build a long term relationship with your Dealership? What are they willing to invest in the relationship? Are they likely to come to you for an oil and filter change or just as likely (or more likely) to visit Jiffy Lube to save a buck or two? Are they more or less likely to fix faulty windshield wipers by going to NAPA Auto Parts or by coming to your service department and waiting for you to fix the problem? If your answers suggest that they are more likely to save a few dollars or do their own repairs or even to skip maintenance altogether, then you need to move on. They are not going to pay more for a relationship with your Dealership.

That leaves the Operational Excellence strategic option. Can a Chevrolet Dealership streamline the buying process to make it hassle-free? Can the Chevrolet Dealership extend its product availability beyond its physical inventory to "virtual inventory" to meet the "Long

Tail" demands of customers? Since price is already transparent on the Internet, can the Dealership provide price transparency on its inventory? Can the Dealership design and execute an online buying process? The answers are yes, yes, yes, and yes.

Now the Tiger Team has a strategy to build around – Operational Excellence. There are probably already many activities going on today in the Dealership that support this strategy. The next step is to conduct a comprehensive inventory to see what needs to change and what can remain the same.

Round 3: What Needs To Get Done

The Tiger Team should start this round by listing at all of your "touch points" – places where your Dealership interacts with your customers. You'll be amazed at how many there are and how each one either adds or subtracts to what you want to be in customer's minds.

The Tiger Team should report back with thoughtful answers the following questions:

- What are all of the customer "touch points"?

- How does the new strategy change each touch point?

- What resources are needed to implement the change? Time? People? Money?

- How will these changes increase revenue and profitability?

- What are the critical success factors that can make or break this solution?

- How will the Dealership make the transition from its current state to this new strategy over the next 30, 60, 90 days?

You'll quickly realize that everything communicates. Everything a Dealership does – from the way it answers the phone, to how long it takes to close a sale, to how the service cashier accepts payment – communicates with the customer. So virtually everything will change to some degree over time.

These changes will create demand for your Dealership and give you a competitive advantage. While every Dealership might sell the same vehicle with the same warranty coverage, if you talk about it in a way that's meaningful to the customer, then you can create demand for your Dealership.

For instance, let's say a new vehicle has a warranty for 5 Years or 60,000 miles. That warranty has no meaning to a customer unless you answer the customer question "so what's in it for me"? Unless there is a direct benefit, it won't create customer demand for the vehicle or your Dealership.

But you can easily translate every product feature to a customer benefit using the simple formula known as "F.A.B." Just use the connecting words "includes" and "so that" to drill down from an uninteresting "thing" to a deep emotional connection.

Feature: 60,000 mile warranty *includes…*

Attribute: bumper to bumper comprehensive coverage *so that*

Benefit: you never have to worry about suddenly coming up with cash or adding to crippling credit card debt.

The Tiger Team should be tasked with recasting each customer touch point as customer benefit. This ensures that every time the customer interacts with your Dealership they know exactly what you stand for and, more important, why they should do business with you and not with the guy across town.

This strategic shift is a process change that must resonate through every fiber of the Dealership to be effective and endure. The Dealer and GM must lead the way and model the behavior they want to see from "greenies" to veterans. Change must come from the top.

But you can and should use your Tiger Team to implement this change. Your Tiger Team has given you the tactical plan to "storm." No one has more ownership than members of the Tiger Team and now is the time for you to exploit their passion.

Courage

At the end of Round 3, your Dealership will be required to show unprecedented courage. Many Dealerships may fear that making changes will turn customers away from your Dealership. In fact, customers will be attracted to your Dealership.

But let's be clear. You will need to start from scratch on some things like your website, sales training, and Fixed Operations processes. By now, you recognize that Objectives drive Strategy and Strategy drives Tactics. Measuring these Tactics drives activity. And therein lies the power of Leadership.

With the proper measurement systems in place, you'll know how to direct activity. More important, you'll know exactly what's working and what's not. Using this intelligence, you'll be able to refine or replace any defective piece of the puzzle.

You might feel like:

- I've already invested too much to change
- I can't get my people to do what they need to do now

- I don't have the time
- I've tried things before and they just don't stick
- Etc., etc., etc.

Ok, but today's environment is different from any other time in the automotive industry. This is a fight for survival. Dealerships are closing every week. Sales and profits are down. Cash is low and getting lower. If you don't want to adapt, then close this book and start to wind down your Dealership or try to sell it at depressed values.

These are painful decisions, but the courageous will make the decisions necessary to get back on track to profitability. This will mean reaching out for help. You will need to work collaboratively within the Dealership, rather than issuing direct commands. And you will need to work collaboratively outside of the Dealership with your Subject Matter Expert vendor partners.

When it comes to technology, you will probably always be at a disadvantage. Gordon Moore, founder of Intel, stated that technology makes a quantum leap every 18 months. As a Dealer, GM or Internet Manager, you simply can't keep up with these changes unless that's the sole source of your livelihood. That means you will have to learn to trust some professional services Subject Matter Experts (SME).

But it also means that leveraging the Intellectual Capital of others will dramatically increase your probability of success and reduce the time necessary to finish the race to your profit destination.

Exercise:

All effective teams must go through the process to "Form, Norm, and Storm." The first step is to form your Tiger Team. List all of the people in your Dealership and you're ready to get busy.

Role	Title	Your Dealership
CEO	Owner	
COO	GM	_____
Tiger Team Leader	Professional Services Integrator	_____
Team Member #1	Internet Manager	_____
Team Member #2	Finance Manager	_____
Team Member #3	Fixed Ops Manager	_____
Team Member #4	Top Salesperson	_____
Team Member #5	BDC Manager	_____
Team Member #6	Website Provider	_____
Team Member #7	CRM Provider	_____
Team Member #8	DMS Provider	_____

8

HOW TO BUILD A
VIRTUAL FOUNDATION

Congratulations. If you've made it this far, you are well on your way
to surviving and thriving in the new customer controlled environment.
By now you've selected a single strategy that is appropriate for each
Dealership store. You've defined all of your touch points. Your
Tiger Team has defined what benefits you want to communicate and
how these benefits will create value in the minds of customers. You
are now ready to build the virtual foundation to deliver at each touch
point to your customers.

The good news is that there is efficiency in building this foundation
for every store and every strategy. Think of how a baker makes cakes.
The baker makes a dozen cakes all from the same batter. Then, he
makes each cake unique, different, and special with the icing that goes
on top.

You can build the same virtual foundation for your Dealership and simply change the "look and feel" of your website, your people, and your service department. These are the three areas to concentrate making changes because these are the areas that make the greatest impact on customers' impressions. This chapter will focus on your website and the subsequent chapters will deal with Fixed Operations and Personnel.

The Website Blueprint

Fortunately for the automotive industry, "Brick and Mortar" retailers have created a clear blueprint of what is necessary to build a solid

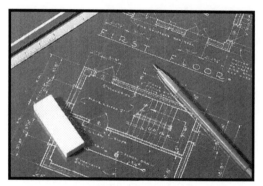

foundation that will open up a new customer demand channel utilizing the Internet.

You'll recall that over 90% of customers use the Internet before they interact with a Dealership. Based on this consistent, predictable customer behavior, AutoTrader.com and Cars.com built a $4 billion dollar advertising industry.

To generate more Internet Leads to sell, Edmunds.com and others are using an aggressive strategy to get their name listed ahead of yours when customers use Google or Yahoo! search engines. This is driving up your pay per click costs, also known as search engine marketing (SEM), and reducing the effectiveness of your organic search engine optimization (SEO) efforts.

But you can change the game by taking a new approach that provides everything these "research" websites offer and more. Specifically, you can create a 24/7 automotive sales solution that automates and micro-manages the last golden mile by creating a "Virtual Showroom."

Just like your Dealership, other "Brick and Mortar" retailers had investments in legacy inventory systems (like your DMS), customer databases (like your CRM), and websites. These retailers learned the hard way that their disparate legacy systems could not provide the "bolt-on" functionality that was required to meet the comprehensive needs of Internet Buyers.

In the end, almost every retailer shifted to a Software as a Service (SaaS) platform that requires no hardware, no software, no training, and no in-house support. These systems simply tap into legacy systems for data and use the SaaS platform in the Internet "cloud" for easy to use functionality, workflow, and business analytics.

A review of the Dealership sales process on the next page shows the progression from the traditional "Brick and Mortar" stage to the current convoluted "Bolt-On" stage. Notice that there are disjointed technologies creating a black hole of customer information.

In contrast, the "Virtual Foundation" starts with your existing Dealership website and connects your CRM and DMS into an integrated system. All customer data is captured and reported in a single data warehouse for easy reporting and automated follow up.

Dealership Technology Evolution

	Build Awareness	Lead Gen.	Set Appts.	Make Selection	Negotiate Price	Assess Trade-In	Sell Financing

BRICK & MORTAR STAGE

			TELEPHONE AND VM SYSTEMS	SHOWROOM SALES TRAINING SYSTEM			DMS SYSTEM

CURRENT "BOLT ON" STAGE

SEM, SEO WEBSITE SYSTEM	3RD PARTY LEAD PROVIDERS	TELEPHONE CRM, ILM SYSTEMS	SHOWROOM SALES TRAINING SYSTEM			DMS SYSTEM

FUTURE STAGE

SEM, SEO WEBSITE SYSTEM	SaaS VIRTUAL SHOWROOM SALES SYSTEM					DMS SYSTEM

Some Dealerships are likely to be concerned about "losing control" of the sales process. Well, remember customers have already taken control on the internet because you have no idea who they are, what they are looking at, when they are looking, and, consequently, you've already lost control.

Traditional retailers have found (and demonstrated convincingly) that there is more sales control when more technology is deployed. By defining the sales transaction process online, retailers can track customers as they move themselves down the sales funnel.

Behavior Tracking (or BT) can tell you for any specific customer what was viewed, when, and how. Behavior Tracking can alert your Dealership in real-time that a specific customer (name, phone number, email, year, make, model) is engaged with your Dealership online. These alerts summarize all behavior for a given customer and can even suggest how to follow up.

This Behavior Tracking capability automates all of the tedious follow up, record keeping, and attention to detail that's expensive to train, manage, and reinforce among salespeople. That's because these activities are usually the weakest skills of salespeople.

Most salespeople like the interaction with the customer. They enjoy the give and take that occurs. They get a thrill out of going for the close. That's what makes them tick. That's what makes them good salespeople. They hate the "administrivia" that technology automates but they love selling which ultimately puts them to their "highest and best use."

Learning From Bugs

Orkin Pest Control figured this sales dynamic out a long time ago. They had an extensive sales force that called on businesses and neighborhoods directly. And their salespeople were dedicated professionals that worked hard at creating demand for Orkin products. Each sales team had a defined geography and they utilized traditional media like TV, radio, print and direct mail to promote their products and services.

For many years, these tactics generated sales traffic for the business. But when the Internet became a pervasive part of life for customers, Orkin saw that these efforts were rapidly becoming less and less effective and watched their sales lead pipeline dry up.

The Orkin management team went to their customer and prospect database and began an email campaign to identify some hot leads to pursue. And here's where they uncovered just how bad salespeople were at keeping accurate, useful, up-to-date data. After hundreds of man-hours to clean and scrub the customer list, Orkin began its efforts to generate sales leads.

Unfortunately, the open rate of these campaigns was almost zero despite increasing the promotion offers to providing services practically for free. When these campaigns did generate a lead, follow up occurred

quickly and frequently by the salespeople, but they simply could not convert interest to sales.

By now, you've seen the parallels with the automotive industry. Advertising doesn't work. Sales pipeline is dried up. Email campaigns don't work. Salespeople can't convert leads to sales.

So what did Orkin do? They started from scratch. They looked at customer behavior to see how customers were purchasing pest control services. People were still buying these services because there are still bugs to kill. Just like people still buy cars because they still need to get from point A to B.

What Orkin learned tells the automotive industry a lot. First, they discovered that when customers purchase pest control services they immediately go to the Internet. Why? Well, when you've got bugs crawling through your business or across your bed at night, that's when you want to do something and do it fast.

So Orkin adapted their sales process to the customer. They used a combination of SEM and SEO to make sure their name popped up whenever any type of bug was entered on a search engine. Then, they rebuilt their website to be a "research" source for all kinds of bugs. This positioned them as Subject Matter Experts (SME's) on the problem.

Then, they directed all customer inquiries to a business development center (BDC) that was staffed 24/7 through a 3rd party. Customers got answers to their questions immediately through iChat, phone, or email – immediately day and night. And these customers spoke to knowledgeable "bug" people who set appointments online for an Orkin service person to meet them at a time that was convenient for the customer, not necessarily Orkin.

The impact was immediate and powerful. Orkin service people received a detailed history of what the customer needed, when they asked for it, and how Orkin had responded so far. They knew exactly how to respond to the customer issues and how the customers felt about the problem. This knowledge powerfully reinforced that Orkin was easy to do business with and was a key factor in building their sales referral business.

In less than a year, Orkin was able to cut their sales force in half while doubling its sales in every market. Marketing expenses also were cut in half since advertising dollars were now redirected to online activities that were much more efficient and cost effective. With lower operating costs and higher revenue, profits soared to the highest levels they've been in the company's history.

Core Components

What does Orkin's experience mean for the automotive industry? To answer that question, let's go beyond Orkin and include a group of hugely successful retailers like Amazon, Apple, Dell, eBay and others who have extensive (and expensive) experience that was acquired through a lot of trial and error.

There are three key lessons learned from these efforts and investments. First, content is king. Second, process is critical. Third, everything must be automated.

Content: Let's start with content. Your website needs to do more than list your inventory. It needs to be surrounded with information about the product much the same way that Amazon provides pictures, video, specifications, manufacturer editorial, and 3rd party editorial reviews.

Amazon learned that customers look for information sources that reassure them about their decision. This is especially true in the automotive industry where trust is low between buyer and seller.

You can build trust with multiple photos of both new and pre-owned vehicles. Use 360° interior and exterior perspectives so customers can conduct a self-directed "virtual walk-around." Tap into the credibility of 3rd party video reviews to give customers a "virtual test drive." These lessons have been proven millions of times over by eBay, AutoTrader.com, Cars.com and others.

But how many Dealership websites tap into the "halo of impartiality" with editorial content aggregated from Car and Driver, NY Times, USA TODAY, Wall Street Journal and other trusted publications? This information is critical in allaying customer fear and building confidence in the purchase.

And how many Dealerships are sharing "Green" environmental ratings, crash test ratings, and other content of keen customer interest. Can customers even compare different vehicles on specifications like customers can do with computers or coffee makers?

And what about customer ratings, not of the Dealership which is often full of unflattering commentary, but of the vehicles that the Dealership is offering for sale? As was previously stated, customers love their vehicle. How have Dealerships tapped into these emotions to persuade other customers to "feel the love" for the vehicles on the lot?

Process: While any website can be loaded full of content, without a clear buying process, these websites are nothing more than "brochure-ware" – pages of words and pictures. These types of websites employ a "Search and Destroy" navigation approach that forces customers to shop in a random, unconnected process.

The key to success of any E-Commerce website is the ease of use and natural navigation that the website provides for the customer. Customers are accustomed to an online shopping process that flows in a step-wise fashion, yet is flexible enough to allow customers to change their minds, skip ahead, or start over.

This is particularly true of a Dealership "Virtual Showroom." Customers seek a familiar, predictable path to follow. But a virtual showroom must provide more than just an intuitive process flow. It must also provide comprehensive customer decision support to build confidence at each step of the buying process.

Dell Computer has mastered this process. Dell took a product category that customers knew very little about and showed them step by step what's important to consider about a computer. Their website is full of "What's this?" links that build customer confidence.

135

Dell built their entire business by shifting responsibility to the customer who was allowed to buy a pre-built computer or customize their computer to meet their unique needs and requirements. Dell did this while simultaneously up-selling more expensive components (e.g., larger hard drives or RAM) and cross-selling additional items (e.g., printers) which customers didn't initially plan on buying. But customers did it because they trusted Dell and paid attention to process prompts that "Purchasers of X also purchased Y."

While Dealerships have albeit a slightly different buying process, customers have the same anxiety and insecurity about purchasing a vehicle as they did before Dell helped them purchase a computer system. Just like Dell, Dealerships can address customer fears and concerns by giving them reasons to believe the Dealership will sell them what they want and need.

On the next couple of pages, there is Table that outlines each step in the E-Commerce vehicle buying process, and the corresponding customer fears and concerns with recommendations on how to overcome these issues. These steps in the buying process and the emotions they elicit come from countless customer qualitative interviews and focus groups.

Process	Fears and Concerns	Reasons To Believe
Why buy from your Dealership?	I want a car, but can I trust you?	We share all vehicle information including pictures, video, reviews, ratings, product evaluations, and "out the door" price.
Inventory	Do you have the car I want?	Here's our entire inventory of new, pre-owned, and certified pre-owned vehicles from all of our Dealership's stores.

Content	Does it have the features I want?	We'll provide for you hundreds of specifications, fuel economy, environmental ratings, crash test ratings and more. You can even do a side by side comparison to see which vehicle best meets your needs.
Price	What's your best price?	Here is our "No Haggle" price with out-the-door detail so there are no surprises.
Accessories	What can I add to customize my vehicle and how much will it cost?	We will show you all of the available Accessories for the vehicle of your choice based on year, make, and model. You can see our pricing and installation fees so there is no misunderstanding.
F&I	How will I know what the warranty covers and what if something happens like I lose my job?	No one can plan for all of life's uncertainty, but we offer extended warranties, gap insurance, and more to give you peace of mind.
Financing	Can I get approved for a loan?	We can let you know all of your finance options before you even come to the Dealership so you'll know all of your options.
Trade-In	How much is my old car worth?	Here is an estimate from an online 3rd party evaluator subject to a physical inspection at the Dealership. In the meantime, download "Selling Your Used Vehicle" to understand the checklist of tasks and risks involved in selling a vehicle.

Automation: The final piece of the puzzle is automation of each step in the buying process. What you are effectively doing through this automation is allowing customers to move themselves down the sales funnel.

Online retailers have automated every step in the process so that customers move themselves from research to product selection to purchase. Most customers will never purchase a vehicle online. Customers usually want to sit in the vehicle, inspect it, and, ultimately take it for a test drive.

But today, these steps are no longer the first steps in the buying process, they are the last steps. If you wait until a customer comes in for a test drive, you've already lost the deal. So you must automate everything and use the customer's efforts to sell for you.

Just like a shopkeeper of an old general store, the new world "Virtual Showroom" must be filled with inventory. Each piece of inventory should include VIN, Stock Number, Year, Make, Model, Mileage, and Price. Fortunately, this inventory can easily be extracted and updated daily from your DMS.

For both new and pre-owned inventory, automated content should be pulled and populated for each Year, Make, and Model. For new vehicles, additional automation should allow the customer to customize exterior color and compare trim packages. For pre-owned vehicles, additional automation should present a 3rd party vehicle history report and new Dealership installed products such as tires, battery, belts, etc.

Price automation should pull M.S.R.P. data, rebates and incentives, your price, and automatically calculate the dollar and percentage discount. (See Chapter 3). Since many customers focus on their monthly payment, an interactive calculator can allow customers to input the amount they want to finance, the length of term, and the interest rate to automatically determine the monthly payment.

Much to the chagrin of Dealers, sales of high margin after-market accessories and add-on Finance and Insurance products during the "Brick and Mortar" transaction process is extremely rare. In contrast, "Virtual Showroom" customers welcome the opportunity to consider additional products from wheels to gap insurance in a "no pressure" environment. Customers can spend time researching the products and calculating the impact on their budget

Finance automation has come a long way in very short time. With a privacy secured application procedure, customers can receive automated loan approvals from 3rd party lenders or directly through the Dealership.

Finally, the trade-in process can also be automated. Customers can enter basic information about their vehicle and instantly receive an estimated value. Of course, the actual trade-in value will be determined at the Dealership.

In the meantime, the customer has moved from being a nameless "Unique Visitor" on your Dealership website to a known Internet Lead. More important, the customer has moved down the sales funnel to setting an appointment without the Dealership lifting a finger.

What To Expect

The initial in-market results of "Virtual Showrooms" have been outstanding:

- Dealership website unique visitor conversion to internet lead increased from 3-5% to 8-10%

- Average time spent in a Virtual Showroom ranged from 4-24 minutes per session

- Number of "click events" in the Virtual Showroom averaged 7 different activities

- Internet Lead to sales conversion increased from industry average of 10-12% to 20-28%

Exercise:

Map the process a customer follows on your website to self-direct themselves down the sales funnel. What Behavior Tracking do you use to alert you a customer walked into your "Virtual Showroom?"

Step	What is customer doing?	How do you know?
1.		
2.		
3.		
4.		
5.		
6.		
7.		
8.		
9.		
10.		
11.		
12.		

9

HOW TO MILK YOUR FIXED OPS CASH COW

You probably know how many sales you want to have this month. You probably also know how many vehicles you sold last month. You may even know where you stand for the year and even how that compares to the same time last year.

But do you know the same sales numbers for Fixed Operations? If not, why not? It's the #1 profit center of the Dealership. It's got the highest margins and the greatest opportunity for both short term and long term growth. What's more, it throws off a ton of cash.

Remember this is one of the levers of your Dealership business. If you have built a "Virtual Showroom," you have already automated your new vehicle E-Commerce sales process to increase your sales velocity while stripping out cost. Deploying this technology allowed you to reallocate your top salespeople to work on another lever of your business, pre-owned vehicles, where interpersonal sales skills are most needed.

In effect, you've reallocated resources to their "highest and best" use. This reallocation of resources (physical, technological, human capital) became famous in 1970's. The Boston Consulting Group (BCG) came up with this concept after reviewing the characteristics of different businesses or business units within a single company.

BCG gave names to these different types of businesses: Stars, Question Marks, Cash Cows, and Dogs. For our purposes, we'll focus on Cash Cows which are defined as businesses with healthy profit margins and an installed base of customers. These businesses are often considered as staid and boring, but their profit and cash contributions make them vitality important. Any company should be thrilled to own a Cash Cow and should milk it continuously.

In fact, Warren Buffet became the world's wealthiest individual (or second wealthiest depending on how the market treats Bill Gates' Microsoft stock) by buying cash cows and milking them for all they were worth. Listen to this list of sexy businesses: Cornhusker Casualty, Waumbec Dyeing and Finishing, Bourne Mills of Canada, Kirkland Reinsurance, K&W Products, Omaha Furniture Mart, and Brown Building Corporation. Most recently, Buffet spent $26.3 billion to buy the Burlington Northern Santa Fe railroad. Not exactly "blue chip, sexy" businesses.

But these ugly businesses were really beautiful on the inside. It just took Warren Buffet to figure out how to make the most of them. In exchange, the businesses made him a multi-billionaire.

Milking The Cow

Now it doesn't take a Warren Buffet to get more out of your Fixed Operations business. It simply takes the same lessons learned from the "front of the store" and applies them to the "back of the store."

Let's start again with a "Virtual Foundation" since the Dealership must still cede control to customers. Only this time, instead of building a "Virtual Showroom" we'll build a "Virtual Parts & Service Department" that taps into social media.

Social media is a perfect way to milk the Fixed Operations cow because social media is designed to be highly accessible and scalable. It's a way for you to transform your Fixed Operations service message monologue (one to many) into a viral social message that can be shared among friends and family (many to many).

This message personalization and endorsement of your Dealership is so powerful that its impact is difficult to estimate. However, in a comprehensive conjoint analysis among 30,000 E-Commerce Internet Leads, the single most powerful way to offset customer interest in Dealerships offering "guaranteed lowest prices" was a positive social media endorsement of your Dealership.

Andreas Kaplan and Michael Haenlein define social media as "a group of Internet-based applications built on the technological foundations of Web 2.0 which allows the creation and exchange of user-generated content."

Kaplan and Haenlein outline the three components of social media:

1. Concept Interest (information)

2. Readily Accessible Media (electronic)

3. Social Interface (viral broadcast)

There are a host of social media companies that have blossomed in the last few years such as LinkedIn (business networking), Facebook (social networking), Twitter (opinion leader following). The strength (and weakness) of these companies is their community policing of content. As any sociologist will tell you, each community has their own set of norms – unwritten rules of what is accepted and what is forbidden.

For Dealerships, these norms are exactly why it's perceived to be inappropriate to "sell" anything utilizing social media. Chris Herman, president of Herman Advertising, says using social media solely for promotional or advertising purposes can be a big mistake. "You turn off anybody who decided to become a fan of your business," he says.

"The most important thing is to establish a relationship with your customer base that's not specifically geared toward promoting product," Herman says. In fact, the number of "fans" on many Dealership Facebook websites grew only after vehicle information was removed and replaced with community news, jokes and other *content that has nothing to do with vehicles*.

A few Dealerships claim that this social media allows them to "sell cars by accident." One Dealership on a social media site told about adopting a stray dog to prevent it from being put down by animal control. They kept the dog not for altruistic reasons, but because the dog chased away raccoons that damaged vehicles in the lot. And one person that came to the Dealership and purchased a vehicle happened to mention that he liked the fact that the Dealership kept the dog.

So which came first? The dog or the sale? It's just like the chicken and the egg. No one really knows. The bottom line is that the Dealership and the customer both pursued their own self-interest. The intersection was indeed by accident. And for a disciplined Marketer, accidents are not a good thing.

AND YET THE QUESTION REMAINED:
"WHO CAME FIRST?"

Think back to the stated purpose of Big "M" Marketing – sell more products to more people for more money. With Social Media, you must have Content Interest first and foremost. If you follow people, ideas, or events you know, then naturally you are interested.

What's so interesting about a Dealership that I would subscribe? What's so fascinating that I would want to contribute? And what's so compelling about the relationship that I would start my vehicle buying process with social media? And as an Internet Manager overwhelmed with responsibilities and activities, what can you promise to deliver to the bottom line? Nothing. Nada. Zip. Zilch.

Double-Edged Sword

Not only is social media incredibly labor intensive, the biggest challenge is that social media is a double-edged sword, especially because users can comment freely about Dealerships. And some manufacturers have been severely stung in social media by naysayers. *And when opinions are written on the Internet, they are written with a pen, not a pencil.*

Linda Gangeri, national advertising manager for Volvo Cars of North America, worries, "People can basically broadcast whatever they want, to whomever they want, whenever they want. We refer to social media as the wild, wild West."

A classic case when things backfired was General Motors' 2006 campaign inviting people to create their own Chevy Tahoe commercials. Although most of the spots were positive, some people posted commercials, often using profane language, criticizing the SUV's fuel economy. Thanks to YouTube, the spots live on, long after the campaign ended and there's no way to stuff the genie back into the bottle.

Honda got slammed recently with negative comments on Facebook about the styling of its Accord Crosstour. A Honda spokesperson said that some comments were based on spy photos purported to feature the Accord Crosstour. It turns out the photos showed a European Accord wagon being used as a mule for power-train development. "We couldn't mess with the site once the comments were there," lamented the Honda spokesperson. "If we took the comments down, we'd never hear the end of it."

While positive comments tend to outweigh negative ones, do you really want to give customers a license to say anything they want about your Dealership? Do you trust people that give themselves monikers like "Knowitall", "HotFlashes46" or "Whatthe****?" to be your Dealership's advocate? What might they say? How would you feel if you couldn't stop their diatribe? Is it a risk worth taking?

Or would you prefer to manage their commentary to increase the probability that social media will be both viral and flattering?

Social Media Playbook

Fortunately, there is a way to manage social media commentary and put it to work to your advantage in a way that is simultaneously flattering and viral. Like many new uses of technology, it's not enough to simply jump on Facebook and start "friending" people. Using social media as a marketing tool to create demand for your Dealership and, specifically your Fixed Operations, requires a new playbook.

This playbook has the same components as an advertising campaign that Nike might create: Media, Message, Creative. For instance, the media might be television advertising on ESPN. The message might be Just Do It! The creative is the actual ad that will get ESPN couch potatoes off their butts and go outside for a run.

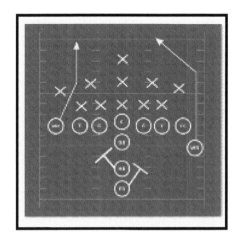

Media:

The most important criteria for the social media that you use for Fixed Operations is that you control it so you can manage the comments that are made about your Dealership. Is it censorship? Absolutely.

If you don't think that companies like Starbucks or Under Armor police what is said about them on their own websites, then you're mistaken. These companies or their marketing agencies routinely remove unflattering comments in order to prevent a single customer or small group of customers from creating an avalanche of negative feedback.

So how do you build social media network that is simultaneously robust and can be easily managed? Well, fortunately the undisputed king of E-Commerce, Amazon.com, will now lease you their technology platform including their administrative controls.

Your Dealership Fixed Operations can build a parts E-Commerce business that includes the social media elements of customer feedback, ratings, and evaluations. Customers can also create their own "Wish Lists" and you can utilize the well known "Customers Who Bought This Item Also Bought" feature to build up their shopping cart.

Most important, you can create an ongoing dialogue with an email campaign full of relevant recommendations based on customers input. This taps into the social media dynamic of creating a more personal dialogue while creating an interesting, engaging, and trusting retail environment.

There is another media that works equally as well on mobile phones. It is a downloadable application for any smart phone like iPhones and Blackberry devices. This two-way application platform asks for the year, model, and mileage in order to proactively provide you with maintenance reminders.

Your Dealership can offer incentives for service, publish warranty information, announce recalls, and even feature streaming video of

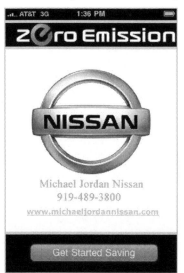

new vehicles. Customers can immediately call for an appointment, email for an appointment or utilize a calendar that's synchronized with your Dealership's open appointment slots.

More important, you can track every customer activity on the application because you have the phone number on the mobile device. The phone number is linked to a specific customer who is linked to a specific vehicle including year, model, and mileage. This information can be used to create a new targeted "Call To Action" that will drive traffic to Fixed Operations.

These new media forms earned entry in the social media playbook for a number of reasons:

1. Simple- easy to use because it's designed for small businesses without IT staff resources

2. Reliable – backed by third-party server farms so no hardware or maintenance needed

3. Powerful – familiar, predictable experience that customers readily embrace

4. Secure – administration controls to manage social media and transaction process flow

Once again, these Marketing activities create demand for your Dealership that's trackable and designed to sell more to more for more.

Message:

As always, we must start with the customer. We need to ask about their needs and wants. We need to understand the value proposition(s) that will get them to change their behavior. We need to find a convenient medium to communicate the Dealership value proposition to customers. And we need a means to immediately act and interact – we need to sell by design, not by accident.

So what is it that customers want? There is a customer insight technique called "Laddering" that continuously asks the question, "Why?" The purpose of the repetitive inquiry is to find the fundamental customer *emotional need* that a product or service satisfies.

For example, people who subscribe to LinkedIn are fundamentally looking for a new job that offers more *security* than they have today. The first Facebook subscribers were college students who posted pictures and personal thoughts protected by the anonymity of the Internet to get *peer approval*. Likewise, single people who subscribe to eHarmony do so to avoid the risk of public rejection and they want *companionship*.

So what in the world to customers want from your Dealership's Fixed Operations? Peer approval? Companionship? Well, not quite, but it's not that far off.

Why do they come today? There are several things that can trigger a visit - a warning light, worn part(s), recall notification, maintenance reminder. What emotion do all of these conditions elicit? *Anxiety*.

Fundamentally, customers are worried that their vehicle will fail when they need it most. So customers come to your service department to relieve their anxiety and re-instill their confidence.

Creative:
In order to stimulate viral distribution, you'll need to focus your creative execution on something that builds on the "What's In It For Me" principle. Customers

will do a lot of things for you if there is something in it for them.

For example, you could stimulate downloads of your Dealership service application on customer smart phones by offering a percentage or dollar discount off today's service. After all, every day you have a captive audience with time on their hands while they wait for their vehicle to be serviced. What better time to build your social media network?

Your creative can help extend your social media network by asking customers to share service reminders with a friend in exchange for discounts off the service for every friend who shows up for a service appointment. You'll know who is eligible for a discount because again you'll be utilizing Behavior Tracking (or BT) to understand everything customers do. When a discount is earned, your Dealership can automatically notify the original customer thanking them for their reference and put a credit in their account for future service.

Before you know it, you'll have friends and family by the thousand engaged with your Fixed Operations. Alerts will go directly to Service Advisors when customers interact with the application. Customers will be prompted to call the Service Department directly from their smart phone. You can even allow customers to set a service appointment online 24/7.

Once again, Marketing will have automated a labor intensive process and stripped out cost. Marketing will have delivered customer demand that can be tracked, measured and managed. And Big "M" Marketing will have allowed you to sell more to more for more while allowing customers to control the process.

Back To The Future

Ironically, social media is using futuristic technology to spread age old "word of mouth" personal recommendations. Many Dealerships were built on personal referrals and these referrals can still work to build profitable demand today.

According to the 2010 Marketing Trends Survey reported by the Center for Media Research, 89% of respondents plan to increase or maintain marketing spending in email campaigns and social media over the next three years. The industry survey of more than 1,000 marketers projected spending to increase 69% for email and 59% for social media. Conversely, spending on marketing events (e.g., tent sales) and direct mail (e.g., service promotion incentives) are projected to decrease spending 44% and 42% respectively.

Respondents identified the top three benefits of social media marketing as:

- Awareness building (64%)
- Customer loyalty and retention (49%)
- Expanded reach (46%)

So go milk that Fixed Operations cow, not by hand, but by utilizing the latest social media technology. But move forward with specific S.M.A.R.T. objectives, stay true to your strategy, and keep your tactical tasks in alignment so your Dealership builds sales intentionally, not by accident.

Exercise:

Calculate how many social media interactions you can achieve in one year using the worksheet below:

Total Number of Service
Appointments Per Year

Download Rate (Based on In-Market Experience)	Multiply by....	.20

Total Number of Social
Network Members

Average Number of Fixed Ops Messages (2 per month)	Multiply by...	24

Total Number of Social
Interactions With Members

Number of Times Message "Forwarded To A Friend"	Multiply by...	2.5

Total Number of Behavior
Tracking Interactions

10

CUSTOMERS ARE JUST NOT THAT INTO YOU

Now that you've decided to build a virtual foundation that will reinvent your Dealership, you have to ask yourself, "How am I going to get it done?" And after I build it, what people do I need to achieve the real goal of sustainable profitability?

Because if you are going to cross a river and you don't have a boat, then you are going to have to build a bridge, buy or rent a boat, or start swimming. If you just stand at the edge of the river and say "Hey, I think I'm going to hang here and read Automotive News and see what happens," the world will pass you by.

And when you are thinking about the resources you are going to need, you also need to think about the people and the skills that you have available. The problem you'll immediately face is that the skills that got you where you are today are not necessarily the skills you will need to get to the next level.

For example, you need a certain set of skills and a specific physical condition to run a 400 meter sprint. But being a great sprinter doesn't mean you can run a marathon. You need to match the skills with the requirements and match the requirements with the compensation.

Think back to what was needed before the internet provided "perfect information" and "price transparency." In the books, *Cars and People: How To Put The Two Together* by Anthony Douglas Ziegler and *From Zero To Hero* by J.F. Knott, the tasks Dealerships needed salespeople to perform included the following:

- Meet & Greet
- Qualify & Conduct Fact-Finding
- Build Rapport
- Vehicle Selection
- Inventory Walk
- Present Product
- Demonstration Drive
- Dealership Tour
- Unmask & Handle Objections
- Write Up
- Negotiate Price
- Overcome Price Resistance
- Conduct Trade-In Appraisal
- Justify Trade-In Value
- Present Financing Options
- Explain Financing Terms & Conditions
- Up-sell Accessories
- Cross-sell Finance & Insurance Products
- Close Deal
- Resell Benefits
- And more....

Salespeople were rewarded for their efforts with generous commissions that allowed salespeople with limited post-high school educations to earn $75,000-$150,000 in good times and bad. Dealerships found well qualified sales candidates and many salespeople remained with a single Dealership for many years.

This steady employment and low turnover encouraged customers to return to the Dealership and buy their next vehicle from a friendly face. This stable relationship encouraged Dealership loyalty because *people are loyal to people, not things*.

And the best salespeople built loyalty and repeat business with birthday cards, hand written letters, and personal phone calls. It was labor intensive, but it used to help sell cars.

Mcdonalds $25/Hour Employees

The problem with hiring, maintaining, and retaining a sales force with these skills is *the Dealership business model no longer can afford it*.

Imagine how great the service would be at McDonalds if you could afford to pay the hourly employees $25 an hour. Unfortunately, the business model of selling fast food at low prices with razor thin margins doesn't allow the business to spend that much for high quality, well trained, self-motivated employees.

This is true for 90% of the foodservice industry. These businesses must adopt a strategy of operational excellence to survive and thrive. They must hire and train people that align with this strategy.

What about the other 10% of the foodservice industry? Well, these restaurants are white tablecloth fine dining establishments where entrées are between $15-35 and the average revenue generated per guest is between $25-50. How much do wait staff earn in these establishments? $25 per hour. Why? Because the white tablecloth fine dining business model can afford it.

Given the razor thin margins on new vehicles, "How much can your Dealership business model afford to pay salespeople?"

Once more, let's turn to the financial statements answer the question. Where does a Dealership make money? How much does it make? And, consequently how much can it afford?

The chart below illustrates what has happened over time to Dealership Net Profits. The trend lines were relatively stable until 2004. What happened? Well, in 2004-2005, every automotive research website like AutoTrader.com, Cars.com, and Edmunds.com began publishing Dealership Invoice Prices. This price transparency coupled with factory incentives like Employee Pricing permanently destroyed profit margins for New Vehicles.

Average Dealer Net Profit

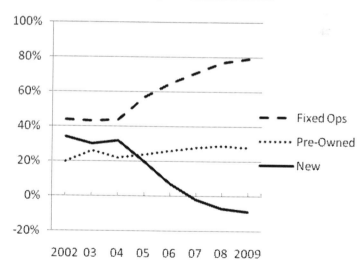

We've already identified that the two levers of the business are Pre-Owned vehicles and Fixed Operations. And we've figured out how to building "virtual foundations" can drive sales and milk Fixed Operations. Now we need to address what the Dealership business model can afford to sell new vehicles.

Fire All Your Salespeople

Should you fire all your salespeople? Before you reject this idea as shear lunacy, let me tell you about a couple of Dealerships that have done just that.

One Dealership sells Toyota vehicles in a suburb of Philadelphia and there is another entire division of a large auto group which owns 100+ stores. These two companies came to the same conclusion about their business model, but arrived there differently.

What's really interesting is that they didn't know what one another was doing and, nonetheless, did the same thing. They started by putting in place a Business Development Center (BDC). What made this BDC unique was that the Dealership decided to hire only women between 35-50 years old and paid them $20/hour without the traditional bonus for "Set Appointments."

These women staffed the BDC from 8am until 10pm. Most of these women are moms with kids at school so getting to the store by 8am was not a problem and staying late was not an issue since most of their husbands took over for them at 5pm.

These women were trained on the different products that they sell at their store. But every Wednesday they go on a caravan just like retail estate agents do to see new houses. Only these women go to other Dealerships to see what's new and customer promotions are available.

Then, they report their findings back on a standardized format which they share with each other. The goal of this exercise is to know what's happening in the local marketplace so they can discuss it with customers and demonstrate their product knowledge. This quickly establishes them as credible resources.

They are tasked with being independent consultants even if that means their store would lose a deal. That's right. If the women at the Toyota BDC talk to a prospect that's interested in a Honda CR-V and a Toyota, they are encouraged (and expected) to direct the prospect to the product and Dealership that is best for the customer.

Why? Because the word of mouth is so powerful that the BDC routinely gets dozens of unsolicited calls every month that turn into Toyota sales at their Dealership. The honesty and integrity of the BDC is what is most important because it becomes a tangible Dealership asset that can be used a million different ways to market and distinguish the Dealership.

What happens next? Well, if the customer is interested in coming to the Toyota Dealership, then an appointment is made. The BDC confirms the appointment 24 hours in advance and will reschedule if necessary.

When the customer arrives at the Dealership, they are greeted with signs that say, "Putting FUN back into buying a car!" The signs explain that no one is on commission and everyone is a Dealership Ambassador to make your visit the best experience you've ever had.

These Dealerships recruit, hire, and train women between 21-28 years of age. Their job description requires them to be ambassadors of the Dealership which includes an attractive personal appearance, strong verbal skills for product presentation, genuine enthusiasm, and strong interpersonal skills.

Consequently, the impact on customers is profound. Young women and men immediately feel like they can relate to their peers. Older women no longer feel intimated by a salesperson trying to control the sale. And older men simply enjoy the attention.

The ambassador is tasked to take the customer through a checklist of activities. Much the same way that a moving company prepares a checklist for moving a household or a business, this checklist is a helpful guide to make sure every item is covered.

And just like a moving company checklist, some items are not relevant and others are extremely important. The magic behind the checklist is that it is a collaborative effort between the customer and the Ambassador.

Once the checklist is completed, the Ambassador asks if the customer would like to purchase the vehicle. If the answer is yes or maybe, then the customer is escorted to a Finance Manager with a guarantee that deal will be done within 30 minutes or the Finance Manager will give the customer an American Express Gift Card of $50 (provided that the customer is a credit worthy buyer.)

This puts the onus on the Finance Manager to make the deal. And the customer is obligated to come pre-qualified or offer the information necessary to be qualified. (By the way, the BDC is tasked with pre-qualifying customers before they come to the Dealership in order to facilitate the Finance Manager's transaction.)

While this is the standard process, it is modified for some customers, particularly customers with questionable credit. In these situations, the customer is escorted by the Ambassador directly to the Finance Manager who can explain the finance options. Of course, the finance options can shift their vehicle preference from a fully loaded option to a base option to the least expensive pre-owned vehicle on the lot. But an educated customer is the best customer.

Likewise, if the customer's trade-in is a large component of the deal, the Ambassador first takes the customer to get an appraisal done. When the appraisal is completed, the presentation of the evaluation includes the Blue Book and Black Book appraisals. It also explains how much the Dealership will invest to close the gap between the two evaluations. Most important, the presentation includes a list of issues for the customer to overcome in a private sale, e.g., placing ads, interacting with unknown buyers, handling insufficient funds, guarding against personal liability, etc.

This is just one example of how customer "touch points" can be utilized to reinforce and communicate your Dealership's value. How you choose to deliver this information will tangibly demonstrate your strategy of Product Differentiation, Customer Intimacy, or Operational Excellence.

165

Nuts And Bolts

To better understand the nuts and bolts of implementing an Operational Excellence strategy within a Dealership, here's an interview with the Internet Director for a Nissan Dealership in the Southeast.

What did you do when you arrived at the Dealership?

I changed everything. There wasn't anything going on that I thought was exceptional so I just dismantled it.

I took the people that were here and said, "Listen, this is what we're going to do. You're going to talk to customers on the phone and respond to their emails. You're going to greet the customers, and you're going to set the appointments. You are going to be the customers' connection."

How do you operate your internet department?

It's set up like a BDC. We've got three coordinators that take care of following up with the customers, setting appointments and handing the deals off when the customers show up at the Dealership. But we don't handle service calls or anything other than satisfying demand for new or pre-owned vehicles.

How do you track and manages leads?

They're entered into the CRM automatically through a tracking number. We get as much information as we possibly can from the customers. Our coordinators discuss:

- customer needs and wants

- what Nissan vehicle customers are looking for

- what other vehicles are under consideration

- if a trade-in is involved

- an appointment for a no-obligation appraisal

- getting loan pre-approval

- pricing posted on Dealership website

- store's unique value proposition

Are you using secure credit applications?

They're one of the main things we focus on with the customer when setting an appointment. We say, "OK, we're going to try to save you as much time as possible and make this as smooth a process as possible. We'd like to get you prequalified before you come in."

Why do you think this automation is so important?

Secure credit applications save us a lot of time. It's easy to set appointments with people that don't have good credit. We explain the secure credit application to our customers and how the automated process will let us give them options on how to structure the deal.

How do you differentiate yourself?

We don't read a script, but there are points of differentiation that make our phone conversations and voicemails stand out. We always provide a "Call To Action" like useful competitive information, special finance rates, manufacturer incentives even gift cards. We are trying to make it worth the customer's time to spend time with us.

What is your experience holding gross?

We average $2,000 a car. So, yes, you can make gross on the internet. But you can't make gross if you're going to shoot out $500 below invoice without trying to brand yourself and give shoppers a reason to do business with you.

What's Lost?

What these Dealerships realized is that they have eliminated a lot of sales tasks. And that's ultimately the job of technology. Automate to eliminate.

With a Virtual Showroom, BDC, and Ambassadors to facilitate the activities at the Dealership, a number of sales tasks have been eliminated or significantly changed.

Let's review the list of sales responsibilities that used to be needed and how they have changed. For instance, the customer has already met and been greeted online where the customer conducted their own self-qualification and fact finding. And there is no need to build rapport or determine vehicle selection or conduct an inventory walk since those activities have already occurred online or else the customer wouldn't be at the Dealership.

The Ambassadors now present the product, conduct test drives, and give dealership tours where they can show up-sell accessories and hand out information on Finance & Insurance products. But the price negotiation, handling objections, trade appraisal, presenting finance options, and closing the deal are shifted to the Finance Manager.

(Most of these responsibilities are already held by the Finance Manager anyway.)

So the question now becomes a different one. Given that the responsibilities of salespeople have been eliminated by technology or replaced by lower cost employees, what do you really need to sell a new vehicle?

And since the profitability of new vehicles has dropped to zero or below zero, what can the business model afford?

What's Gained?

The Dealerships smart enough to "fire all of their salespeople" have gained a tremendous amount even during difficult economic times. Here's a partial list of what they've gained in a short period of time:

- Increased sales 5% vs. industry decline 20-40%
- Averaged $1,500-2,500 gross profit on new vehicle sales
- Reduced operating expenses 30%
- Reduced advertising expenses 30%
- Reallocated 50% of advertising expenses to online activities
- Limited turnover to 15% with full-time employees

There are a host of gains that are more difficult to quantify. These Dealerships report a much higher level of enthusiasm and teamwork. The GM's uniformly report a palpable sense of pride of ownership within the Dealership and more affection between customers and the Dealership.

In fact, several GM's told stories about customers who insisted on meeting the kind, thoughtful woman from the BDC that they'd spoken to on the phone and online. When they met, the customers gave hugs to these women who they thought of as friends and neighbors.

Now, there aren't enough Little League teams and school fundraisers in the world to engender that kind of response. It came from giving up sales control in order to gain sales control.

And gaining sales control is still the name of the game. What's changed is how you get it.

What Can Stay The Same

Making such a radical change is probably not something most Dealerships feel comfortable embracing. And there is a middle ground. (At least for the next 18-24 months, then all bets are off.)

As previously discussed, pre-owned vehicle sales are a lever of the Dealership business model. Specifically, there is more profit to be made on pre-owned vehicles so there is more room for sales commissions to be paid. In other words, the pre-owned business can afford it.

And selling pre-owned vehicles requires more sales skills since there is inherently even less trust between buyer and seller. Customers want to know about the vehicle's history, what's been done to improve its performance, what's covered under the manufacturer's warranty, what's covered under the Dealership's warranty, and more.

While many of these processes can be (and should be) automated online, pre-owned customers inevitably want to see the vehicle's condition and make their own evaluation of how the vehicle might fit their needs.

This is where the talent of salespeople can be put to good use. It is important to establish rapport and develop trust that the vehicle will perform as expected and last as long as projected. This is very different from new vehicle sales where vehicles from the factory are the same.

One large Dealership group goes a step further with its sales efforts and provides a "Rest Easy" kit with every pre-owned vehicle. Included in the kit:

- Manufacturer Warranty

- Dealership Warranty

- Dealership Reconditioning

- Carfax Report

- Inspection Checklist

- Gap Insurance

What makes this "Rest Easy" program come to life is the delivery of the kit on a goose down-stuffed pillow. It tangibly demonstrates the "Rest Easy" value proposition and communicates throughout the entire Dealership the importance of removing anxiety from the buying process.

Taking the middle ground allows the Dealership to retain its highest performing and most valuable salespeople while jettisoning the rest. These salespeople will earn more while turning inventory at a higher rate. Likewise, the Dealership will earn more from a lower cost structure and increased sales velocity.

Different Plans, Different Resources

Regardless of whether the Dealership stakes out the high ground or claims the middle ground, there is one thing that simply must change – your Internet Manager's role and responsibility.

Think about it. The Dealership has invested millions on its "Brick and Mortar" store and continues to pour tens of thousands of dollars into the facilities every month. Now, the Dealership is going to invest in a

"Virtual Showroom" that represents the way that 90+% of customers first interact with your Dealership.

The Internet Manager is effectively becoming the General Sales Manager of the online store. The Internet Manager is responsible for driving traffic to the site, making sure the site is inviting, providing compelling reasons to do business, converting unique visitors to leads, managing those leads down the sales funnel, qualifying their ability to buy, and convert leads to sales.

Yet, the majority of the compensation earned by Internet Managers' comes from the number of vehicles they sell. There's not enough time in a day to do what needs to be done and still produce the results that you want. It's like asking nine women to get pregnant for a month in order to have a baby. It can't be done.

More important, the business model can't afford it. You cannot afford for the Internet Manager to be distracted from anything other than creating demand for your Dealership and your products and services. This position must be a full-time employee position with a salary of $75,000-100,000 plus benefits.

The Internet Manager also must be part of the Dealership Management team. They need to know about sales targets, Dealer incentives, aging inventory, profit goals and other key metrics. And it's absolutely critical that they have a budget with profit and loss responsibility.

Some job positions have a natural progression within the Dealership. For instance, some salespeople can be groomed for General Sales Manager roles and may later be develop as GM's. But if you are charting a new course to build a Virtual Showroom replete with new

173

sales processes and new marketing tactics, then you cannot fill that role with a salesperson that "gets" computers.

You need to hire a professional Marketer with an entirely different set of skills than what you had before. You need people with experience converting large scale initiatives into action. They need change management abilities, process improvement skills, and capabilities to profitably drive the bottom line.

You may already have that person in your Dealership. If you do, then you are very fortunate. You need to immediately reward this person with a new title, new salary, and new responsibilities commensurate with your new expectations.

What's most important is that this person has a deep understanding of the customer and customer behavior as it specifically relates to the buying process. This person will understand that customers aren't that into you. It's their job to turn cynical, distrustful customers into loyal, die-hard fans.

And that ain't easy.

Exercise:

"Automate to Eliminate" is the job of technology and high performing personnel. Rank the top 5 items you'd like to eliminate (or at least substantially reduce) at your Dealership.

<u>Ranking</u>

Employee Turnover

Employee Hiring   _____

Employee Training   _____

Employee Absenteeism   _____

Employee Compensation Complaints   _____

Poor Technical Skills   _____

Poor Interpersonal Skills   _____

Poor Writing Skills   _____

Poor Follow Up Skills   _____

Poor Customer Documentation Skills   _____

Poor Reporting Skills   _____

                                                    _____

PART 4
MEASURE, REFINE, REPEAT

11

RESULTS: IS THIS STUFF REALLY WORKING?

Dealerships are notorious for measuring all kinds of things. But being notorious is not a complement. Merriam-Webster defines "notorious" as a widely known unfavorable indictment.

Don't misunderstand me. A lot of Dealership measurements are great – number of appointments, number of appointment shows, number of units sold. And some Dealerships drill down further and measure traffic, deals lost to bad credit, and the number of "Be Backs." These efforts are absolutely critical because all that matters at the end of the day is driving profitable sales.

And that's where the conundrum lies. When I visit Dealerships, they can tell me how many units they've sold and how much money they are losing or making. *But they can't tell me why.*

The obvious answers come quickly. Expenses are greater than revenues. Gross margins are slim or non-existent. Floor-plan costs are out of control. Then, the obvious follow-up question comes: What are you going to do about it?

Dealership Demand

So how does a Dealership measure demand? Do you know how many unique visitors visit your website each month? Do you know your conversion rate from your website to internet lead? Do you know your internet lead conversion rate to sales for the leads originating from your website?

Do you know how many contacts it takes to make an appointment? Do you know how many of these contacts are online and how many are off-line like phone calls? Do you know how many credit applications you pre-qualify per month? Do you know how many of these qualified customers show up at the Dealership? Do you know how many of these qualified customers buy?

All of these questions are measurements of demand for your Dealership and your products. All of your marketing efforts should be specifically designed and executed to drive demand. And you spend tens of thousands of dollars every month. *Do you know what you get for that investment?*

Here are some benchmarks that you can use for a self-assessment. (Benchmarks are monthly metrics.)

Demand Metric	Industry Benchmark	Best In Class Dealerships	Your Dealership
Website Unique Visitors	3,000	5,000	
% Unique Visitor to Internet Lead	3-4%	8-12%	
# Website Internet Leads	90-120	400-600	
% Internet Lead Appt.	30%	75%	
# of Internet Lead Appts.	27-36	300-450	
% Internet Lead Appt. Shows	50-67%	75%	
# Internet Leads Appt. Shows	14-24	225-337	
% Internet Lead Appt. Shows Sales Conversion	50-67%	75%	
# Internet Leads Sold	7-16	168-253	
% Internet Lead Sales Conversion	8-13%	42%	
# Internet Leads Blown Thru	83-104	232-347	
% Internet Lead Blow Thru Rate	92-87%	58%	

Make R.O.I. Your Best Friend

Setting a budget may be one of the most subjective, frustrating business processes you'll ever face. Most Dealerships patch together a loose formula based on expenses, the company's financial situation, and the Dealer's or GM's mood at the time.

In theory, there are all sorts of complicated ways to figure out your budget. Forget the academics. Let common sense drive your spending decisions. There are some trackable activities that create and manage demand for your Dealership and your products and services. The rest is fluff.

Here's the short list for vehicle sales:

Key Metric	Target	Who's Responsible
Unique Visitors Searching Inventory	3,000 Per Month On New and Pre-Owned Landing Page	Website Provider
New and Pre-Owned Vehicle Internet Leads	10% Unique Visitor to Internet Lead Conversion Rate	Virtual Showroom Provider
Pre-Owned Vehicle Internet Leads	1 Credit Worthy Lead Per $20 Invested	Lead Providers
Email Open Rate; Click Thru Engagement Rate	40% Open Rate; 40% Click Thru; 40% Multi-Click Thru	Internet Lead Management
Outbound Calls To New and Pre-Owned Prospects	10 Calls Per Month with 2 Calls To Action Per Message	BDC

Let's take a look at your website and determine your budget using these metrics. If the market rate for a Internet Lead from your Dealership website is $60 per Lead* and you get 3,000 unique visitors on your website with a 10% unique visitor to internet lead conversion rate, then your budget for your website is 300 Internet Leads @ $60 each or $18,000.

(*Assumes Average 3rd Party Cost Per Internet Lead = $20; Dealership Website Leads 3 Times More Likely To Buy = $60)

Then calculate your Return On Investment (R.O.I.) which should be 3-5 times your marketing investment. Of these 300 Internet Leads, you should sell to 20% or 60 vehicles. If the gross profit of each vehicle is $1,500, then you will generate $90,000 profit. Your marketing R.O.I. is $90,000 divided by $18,000 or 5 times your investment.

Obviously, if any of these variables change, then your R.O.I. will change. You'll have to either improve your demand generation performance or lower your costs. The easy way out is to lower your costs but that will defeat your goal of driving customer demand. Remember you get what you pay for. You can't buy a Porche for $5,000 and you can't get great performance from a lousy product.

When you make R.O.I. the measuring stick, then you'll have a strong business case to defend to anyone, including your website provider. Who will know exactly what needs to be delivered – Return On Investment.

Are You With Us Or Against Us?

Unless R.O.I. metrics are jointly established, neither your Dealership nor your vendor partners will know how well they are performing. Without feedback, no one knows how to improve so everyone stays on the treadmill working hard, but going nowhere.

Soon the relationship will erode until the question pops out, "Are you with us or against us?" Sadly, I don't know why so many Dealerships assume such an adversarial attitude so quickly.

Perhaps the problem stems from long-term contracts gone bad. In these cases, there is often an initial honeymoon followed by some Dealership turnover and some vendor partner neglect. Soon both sides feel like the relationship is not all they were promised or expected.

Fortunately for everyone involved, most of these long-term contracts have morphed into annual agreements or even month to month arrangements. Still there seems to be distrust between buyer and seller. Just as Dealership salespeople become frustrated with customers who seem evasive or misleading so do vendor partners. The vendors really do want to help you grow your sales and profits because they know that if they aren't part of the solution to your problems then they will be out of the door.

One way to ensure that both sides are aligned is to set S.M.A.R.T. objectives for every month. This forces both Dealership and vendor partner to agree on what should be accomplished together. Then, it is the vendor partner's responsibility to track, measure, and report how the vendor partner performed against these objectives.

Likewise, the Dealership must share performance data with the vendor partner. Usually it is little more than units sold (new vs. pre-owned) by salesperson with gross per unit. Some Dealerships may bristle at giving out this information, but unless tangible results are shared, then the vendor partner is left in the dark about how to improve their performance to benefit the Dealership.

A second way to get alignment between Dealership and vendor partner is to formally include a certain number of professional services hours in the agreement between the parties. The vendor partner is responsible for fulfilling those hours in the capacity that the Dealership reasonably requests to improve the Dealership performance. This may take the form of training new employees, advising on new technology, conferring on strategy, or mystery shopping customer "touch points."

Finally, both Dealership and vendor partner should schedule quarterly "top to top" meetings between the senior management of both parties. The agenda for these meetings should be to review the S.M.A.R.T. objectives and performance against these objectives. The vendor partner should be prepared to discuss new ways to improve performance, new product developments, and a competitive overview of the market for the Dealership. In turn, the Dealership should be prepared to provide sales performance, fact-based performance issues or concerns, and a direction for the next quarter.

But the most important elements of the relationship is attitude and effort. Like any relationship, it will blossom and flower with care and attention. The attitude must be one of joint venture and mutual respect. The effort must be earnest and sincere.

This doesn't mean all relationships will work out. (Think back to your dating history.) But it does mean that it is more likely to be mutually beneficial. And in the business world, mutually beneficial translates into more money for everyone.

Myths To Be Debunked

There seem to be a lot of myths about software vendor partners in particular that need to be clarified before a healthy relationship between Dealership and software vendor partners is possible.

I'm going to give you an inside look at how software companies make and lose money. Hopefully, a peek behind the curtain will lend some perspective to the classic conversations Dealerships and software vendor partners have every day:

Dealership: How much will it cost?

Software Guy: It depends on what you need.

Dealership: How will I know until I try it?

Software Guy: What do you need to try?

Dealership: Everything. Give me a free trial.

Software Guy: For how long?

Dealership: Until I know it works.

Software Guy: How will you know?

Dealership: I'll know it when I see it.

Now we're talking about software here, not pornography! This conversation is one I always want to flip back to the Dealership and reverse our roles. I'd say to the Dealership, "Yes, I'd like a car, but I'd like to drive it for free and I'll return to pay for it when I know that it works for me." How many Dealerships would accept those terms?

Dealerships need to be specific about what they want to see happen. (What benchmarks must be achieved? What R.O.I. is required? What key metrics must be tracked?) Then the software vendor partners can decide whether they can deliver against your detailed requirements or walk away. No software vendor partner wants to make you unhappy, especially with public blogs and postings that can destroy a vendor partner's reputation.

Use demos, case studies, reference clients to assess if the software vendor partner is the right fit for your Dealership. Then make a decision and move forward with a month to month contract. Or choose a longer term for a reduced rate.

The worst thing you can do is an extended "trial." You'll never be truly committed to the product and the software vendor partner will never be truly committed to you. With nothing to lose, there's no urgency to implement, refine, and optimize to make sure the investment is worthwhile.

187

Here are some specific myths that need to be debunked:

Myth #1   *If I reveal my budget, the software vendor partner will take advantage of me.*

Truth: Withholding information about your budget is waste of everyone's time. You would never try to sell a car without understanding someone's budget. How can a software vendor partner make intelligent recommendations about the best way to meet your needs if it doesn't understand your budget?

Myth #2:   *Software vendor partners are obscenely profitable so they can afford to give me a deep discount.*

Even the smallest software vendor partner invests millions and millions of dollars years before they generate the first dollar of revenue. The average pre-tax profit for a mid-sized software vendor partner in the U.S. is 15.8%. It only takes a few slow or non-paying Dealerships to have a serious impact on a software vendor partner's financial health.

Myth #3   *We don't have a budget.*

It's amazing how many Dealerships say this and really believe it. They may not have a formal budget, but whether they realize it or not, they sure do have a spending threshold. If the software vendor partner creates a zero-based recommendation and it violates that threshold, you can hear the shouting from the street, "It costs how much? You know we can't afford that!"

Myth #4: *I can get the same thing from somewhere else for half the cost.*

No matter what the software does, you can get something for half the price from someone else. In fact, you can get something for a tenth of the price. The key words here are "the same capabilities." Every software product is different just like every vehicle is different. Some software is very similar to other software, just as some vehicles are very similar to other vehicles. But no software does the "same thing."

Myth #5: *We can do it for less in-house.*

This one always cracks me up. No you can't. Not now, not ever. Every software vendor partner has dozens if not hundreds of programmers, massive server farms, and millions of lines of code. Even a "simple" iPhone application running on a single carrier network (AT&T) has to be backwards and forwards compatible with multiple operating system versions.

Myth #6: *Software vendor partners inflate their prices because they expect us to negotiate. If we don't push back, then we're leaving money on the table.*

There are some costs like set-up fees that can be waived in order to expedite the sale. But just like the Dealership doesn't like to get nickel and dimed on a vehicle deal, neither does a software vendor partner. Ironically, the Dealerships that work so hard to beat software companies down to a pulp are the same Dealerships that hate customers that do the same thing to them. Matthew 7: 12 – "Do unto others, as you would have them do unto you."

Myth #7:	*If you give a discounted rate to my store, I will help you get into the other stores in the Dealership group.*

Almost always untrue. Each store is a multi-million dollar business unit with independent GM's and Internet Managers responsible for their own P&L. Even when Dealers want the software in all stores, there is still a huge sales, training, and support expense associated with each store.

And once you discount your product, you will never be able to raise the price for the other stores to recoup your losses.

Myth #8:	*We just need you to make a few changes. Why can't you do it?*

What you think are a "few changes" might impact thousands of lines of code. Even if these changes are made, the software vendor partner has to support and maintain multiple versions. Multiple versions create multiple problems. Multiple problems create systemic breakdowns. Systemic breakdowns upset customers. Upset customers create cancelled agreements. Cancelled agreements put the vendor partner out of business. 'Nuff said.

Ten Commandments For Failure

There are a number of recommendations and suggestions in this book. If you follow the advice, you will certainly be successful. But as mentioned in Chapter 4, sometimes it's easy to think about what you don't want to happen rather than what you should do.

The Ten Commandment for Business Failure by Don Keough, former
president of The Coca-Cola Company, writes about what he believes
are the ten commandments that will guarantee failure for everyone.
Even though Coca-Cola is the most recognized brand on earth, it is
still vulnerable to failure. Take these lessons as a cautionary tale.

Commandment One: Quit Taking Risks
"You've always done it this way. Quit taking risks. Now's not the
time to try something different."

Commandment Two: Be Inflexible
"When the conditions around you change, remain inflexible. Keep on
keeping on. Stand firm."

Commandment Three: Isolate Yourself
"Don't make the boss mad. Bring no bad news. And no new ideas."

Commandment Four: Assume Infallibility
"If something seems to be heading in the wrong direction, cover up
and hunker down until it gets better."

Commandment Five: Play the Game Close to the Line
"Be sure to cut every corner, use every loophole, and take every
opportunity to take advantage of your business partners, but leave an
opening to blame them when you fail."

Commandment Six: Don't Take Time to Think
"Obsess over the latest technology. But don't spend time thinking
about what you want it to do."

Commandment Seven: Put All Your Faith in Experts
"Be sure to play follow the leader. They must know what they are
doing."

Commandment Eight: Love Your Bureaucracy

"Love command and control hierarchy and guard it with your life because any change might undermines your power or authority."

Commandment Nine: Send Mixed Messages

"It doesn't matter what you do, you'll be rewarded just for being here."

Commandment Ten: Be Afraid of the Future

"Don't push any new idea forward. It's better to be miserable because in some perverse way it makes you feel safe."

Don Keough was trying to make a point that should not be missed. He was articulating the symptoms of the Pretend-It's-Not-There syndrome. These are the one or two collective weaknesses that nobody talks about (not in public, anyway).

These weaknesses are the things that keep you up at night and the obstacles you must overcome before you can be successful. You must deal with these issues before any positive change is possible. Ask yourself:

- If our Dealership failed tomorrow and we could overhear our closest competitors gossiping about it, what would they say?
- If new investors took over this Dealership tomorrow, what would they change first?

Don't let your Dealership's epitaph be on this list:

- We should have tried something different.
- We should have asked for help.
- We bought the cheapest, but needed the best.
- We lost our courage to change.
- We gave up too soon.
- We worried about making a mistake.

Now a lot of things I am suggesting might seem like just common sense. But when you start to implement them, you are going to be considered a trailblazer, not someone who merely paved over the well-worn goat paths.

So take pride and pleasure in striving to be better and innovating with abandon. You'll be in the company of great adventurers like Teddy Roosevelt who said:

> *"It is not the critic who counts. The credit belongs to the man who is actually in the arena, whose face is marred by dust and sweat and blood; who strives valiantly, who comes short again and again, because there is no effort without error and shortcoming; but who does actually strive to do the deeds; who knows great enthusiasms, the great devotions; who spends himself in a worthy cause; who at the best knows in the end the triumph of high achievement, and who at the worst, if he fails, at least fails while daring greatly, so that his place shall never be with those cold and timid souls who neither know victory nor defeat."*

12

WHO YA GONNA CALL?

So now I've given you a long list of what needs to be done to adapt to the customer controlled automotive industry. This is an arduous set of tasks, but with professional assistance you can get everything completed in a matter of a few months. That's a short timeframe for completely revamping your Dealership business model.

But the transition can occur quickly because the strategic hard work is already done. The software capabilities you need already exist. The sales process road map is complete. It's just up to you to adapt these tools for your Dealership.

You have to:

FORM	1. Create a Tiger Team
NORM	2. Define Where You Are Today
	3. Determine Your "Go To Market" Strategy
	4. Outline What Needs To Change
	5. Build A Virtual Foundation
	6. Create Fixed Operations Social Media Community
STORM	7. Hire, Train, and Inspire New Organization

8. Establish Performance Benchmarks
9. Set Monthly S.M.A.R.T. Objectives
10. Calculate R.O.I.

By now, you're probably thinking, "who can I call to help me?' You just told me to completely transform my business model to be more profitable, efficient, and effective. Who is going to do it? There's only one of me!

Well, like most business opportunities, you have an option to build or buy. If you build a Marketing organization, then you need to fill it with good people and they are expensive. Since your business model doesn't allow you to build, then you must buy or at least rent the "Subject Matter Expertise" that you need.

Here is a list of "car guys" who understand the future of the automotive industry and can help you get there. These guys should be the professional services leaders of your Tiger Team discussed in Chapter 7:

SME	Contact Info	Experience
Steve Stauning	Kain-Stauning Pladoogle.com Atlanta, GA Steve@kainstauning.com 404-840-3493	Reynolds and Reynolds; Asbury E-Commerce
Tom Fee	Verity Partners Atlanta, GA tfee@veritypartnersllc.com 404-229-9490	Booz Allen Consulting Deloitte Consulting AutoTrader.com Consultant
David Kain	Kain Automotive Lexington, KY david@kainautomotive.com 859-533-2626	Dealer Principal; Founder, Ford Direct.com

If you want to do-it-yourself (DIY), here are folks you'll need to contact to build your "Virtual Showroom" Discussed in Chapters 8.

SME	Contact Info	What you need
Mike Lefteris	AutoData Troy, MI Michael.lefteris@autodata.net 519-282-5260	Vehicle Specs M.S.R.P. Incentives/Rebates Editorial Reviews
	Black Book	Trade-In Evaluator
	Chrome	Vehicle Editorial Videos (Models 2006-Present)
	eVox	Colorized Images 360 Interior/Exterior
	IBM Cognos 866-601-1934	Business Intelligence
	Limelight	Internet Edge Video Streaming
	Rackspace	SQL Databases Application Hosting
	PayPal	Secure Payment Infrastructure
	VeriSign	SSL Certification ID Encryption

If you want to do-it-yourself (DIY), here are folks you'll need to contact to build your "Virtual Parts & Service Department" discussed in Chapters 9.

SME	Contact Info	What you need
Amazon.com	www.Amazonservices.com	Website By Amazon Amazon Payments Checkout By Amazon Amazon Simple Pay
Mark Morel	Whoop! Everything Mobile Atlanta, GA InfoWhoop@whoop.com 1-877-88Whoop	Content Creator Content Publisher Content Distributor Unique ID Per Store Unique Merchandise Unique Tracking

And, of course, if you want to chat about anything in this book, email kurt@marketsquaresolutions.com or give me a call 678-460-0400.

I'll be happy to serve as a professional services leader of your Tiger Team, evaluate technology solutions against your requirements, and/or help integrate your disparate IT systems. Lastly, I'm always available as a "Big M" Marketer to drive customer demand for your Dealership!

Frequently Asked Questions

Dealerships looking to adapt their business model are often curious about what it's going to take to change in terms of time, people, and, of course, money. These answers should give you some perspective of the investment required of your Dealership.

Q: **This seems like a lot of work. How long will it take to implement from start to finish?**

A: There are three key phases of work: 1). Tiger Team assessment; 2). Vendor Partner Integration; 3) Dealership Training & Roll-out. Each phase will take about 30 days so approximately 90 days of hard work.

Q: **I still have to run the Dealership. How am I going to find the time to do all of this work?**

A: The easiest way to complete the work is to hire a Professional Services Consultant since Dealership change management is their expertise. And don't forget your vendor partners (SME's) can step in and do a lot of the work for you as well.

Q: **How much does a Professional Services Consultant cost?**

A: Professional Services Consultants usually bill $175-$225 per hour, but you can get a much lower rate if you contract for the entire project.

Q: **How much will building the "Virtual Foundation" cost?**

A: If you build it from scratch, it will probably cost $200-300k. The far better option is to pay a Software as a Service (SaaS) vendor partner $3-4k per month for everything you need.

Q: **How much will the "Virtual" Fixed Operations Parts and Service E-Commerce system cost?**

A: The monthly fee from Amazon is approximately $1k per month, but the build out with all of your parts will cost about $100-200k. Again, it's much more cost effective to pay a Software as a Service (SaaS) vendor partner $2-3k per month.

Q: **How much will it cost to train my people throughout the year?**

A: If you negotiate quarterly training in your agreements with software vendor partners, then training should be at no cost.

Afterword

Books are good enough in their own way, but they are a mighty bloodless substitute for living.

- Robert Louis Stevenson

Thank you for reading my book. This took an investment of both your time and your energy. In return, I hope that you've gained insight into how to change your Dealership business model to adapt to the customer controlled Internet environment.

I also hope to meet you someday. If you have this book lying around, hopefully you can show me how you took notes, dog-eared pages, underlined text. Nothing is more flattering to an author than to see his book has been "used."

From time to time, please check www.MyDealerBroadcast, because I will upload Dealership case studies, whitepapers, templates, and other resources for your use.

Now get busy. There's no time to waste. The world is rapidly changing around you. You have a simple choice to make for your Dealership – Adapt. Or Die.

Bibliography

Ariely, Dan. Predictably Irrational: The Hidden Forces That Shape Our Decisions. New York: Harper-Collins, 2008.

Clancy, Kevin J. and Robert S. Shulman. Marketing Myths That Are Killing Business: The Cure For Death Wish Marketing. New York: McGraw-Hill, 1993.

Coleman, Chris. The Green Banana Papers: Marketing Secrets For Technology Entrepreneurs. Atlanta: St. Barthelemy Press, 2001.

Eades, Keith and James Touchstone and Timothy Sullivan. The Solution Selling Fieldbook: Practical Tools, Exercises, Templates, and Scripts For Effective Sales Execution. New York: McGraw-Hill, 2005.

Godin, Seth. Purple Cow: Transform Your Business By Being Remarkable. New York: Penguin Books, 2003.

Gross, T. Scott. Positively Outrageous Service: The Ultimate Antidote For Today's Tough Times: How To Surprise And Astound Your Customers And Win Them For Life. New York: Warner Books, 1991.

Knott, J.F. From Zero To Hero: How To Master The Art Of Selling Cars. New York: iUniverse Star, 2007.

Lenskold, James D. Marketing ROI: The Path To Campaign, Customer, And Corporate Profitability. New York: McGraw-Hill, 2003.

Nalebuff, Barry and Ian Ayres. Why Not? How To Use Everyday Ingenuity To Solve Problems Big And Small. Boston: Harvard Business School Press, 2003.

Treacy, Michael and Fred Wiersema. The Discipline Of Market Leaders: Choose Your Customers, Narrow Your Focus, Dominate Your Market. Boston: Addison-Wesley Publishing Company, 1995.

Von Oech, Roger. A Whack On The Side Of The Head: How You Can Be More Creative. New York: Warner Books, 1990.

Weissman, Jerry. In The Line Of Fire: How To Handle Tough Questions When It Counts. New York: Prentice Hall, 2005.

Ziegler, Anthony Douglas. Cars and People: How To Put The Two Together. New York: iUniverse Star, 2007.

Zyman, Sergio. The End Of Marketing As We Know It. New York: Harper Business, 1999.

Index